Y0-BYA-477

SYBASE® Replication Server™ Primer

McGraw-Hill Series-Computer Communications

TCP/IP Networking: A Guide to the IBM Environment by *Peterson*

Enterprise Network Performance Optimization by *Nemzow*

Wireless Local Area Networks: Technology, Issues, and Strategies by *Davis, McGuffin*

ISDN Computer Applications Development by *Hutchinson*

The ODBC Solution: Open Database Connectivity in Distributed Environments by *Signore, Creamer, Stegman*

Writing VX-REXX Programs by *Richardson*

Linking LANs—2nd Edition by *Schatt*

TCP/IP and Related Protocols—2nd Edition by *Black*

Network Management Standards: OSI, SNMP, and CMOL Protocols —2nd Edition by *Black*

The V Series Recommendations—Standards for Data Communications Over the Telephone Network—2nd Edition by *Black*

Electronic Mail Systems: A Network Manager's Guide by *Fatah*

SYBASE® Replication Server™ Primer

Charles B. Clifford

McGraw-Hill, Inc.

New York San Francisco Washington, D.C. Auckland Bogotá Caracas Lisbon London Madrid Mexico City Milan Montreal New Delhi San Juan Singapore Sydney Tokyo Toronto

hc 1 2 3 4 5 6 7 8 9 DOC/DOC 9 0 0 9 8 7 6 5

Library of Congress Cataloging-in-Publication Data
Clifford, Charles B.
SYBASE replication server primer / by Charles B. Clifford.
p. cm.
Includes index.
ISBN 0-07-011515-X (H)
1. Relational databases. 2. Sybase. 3. Client/server computing.
I. Title.
QA76.9.D3C55 1995
005.7'58—dc20 95-18169
CIP

Acquisitions editor: Jennifer Holt DiGiovanna
Editorial team: Robert E. Ostrander, Executive Editor
Aaron G. Bittner, Book Editor
Production team: Katherine G. Brown, Director
Alan Bookmiller, Computer Artist
Jan Fisher, Desktop Operator
Design team: Jaclyn J. Boone, Designer
Katherine Lukaszewicz, Associate Designer

GEN1
011515X

To my daughter Brittany.
May you practice good, avoid evil, and do good for others.

Acknowledgments

Over the past couple of years I have had the opportunity to work with a number of talented colleagues and clients. As we have worked together with (and on) the SYBASE Replication Server, they have taught me many important lessons about this technology and its application to business problems.

Also, some of them have raised tough questions about this product, questions that would never have occurred to me. But by struggling to find answers to their questions, I have learned from their inquiries.

My thanks to all of you.

Contents

6 Stable Queues *51*

7 Replication definitions and subscriptions *67*

Introduction

The purpose of this SYBASE Replication Server Primer is to shed light on the nature of, and on the relationships that exist between, the SQL Servers, Log Transfer Managers, Replication Servers, and the Replication Server Manager that make up a typical SYBASE Replication system.

Here in the West, we are trained to view things as independent and isolated entities. This cultural predisposition is a real barrier to realizing that all of these components participate within the Replication system in a mutually interdependent manner. However, this mirage is a useful way of separating figures from their ground so that we can dissect them, and see what makes them tick.

To successfully design, develop, test, and deploy a SYBASE Replication system, you will have to simultaneously hold the big picture in mind while you focus on the minute details. It is hoped that this book will help you accomplish both goals.

1

Overview of the SYBASE Replication Server

This chapter presents an overall survey of the SYBASE Replication Server, its functions, and issues related to those functions.

Data and transaction integrity issues within a distributed database system

There is a lot of ambiguity surrounding the topic of distributed computing systems in general, and distributed databases in particular. Volumes have been written about distributed computing systems, and more will be written still. In order to settle the waters somewhat, a distributed database system is being defined as a computing system that contains a number of autonomous database management systems (not necessarily all SYBASE SQL Servers) that are interconnected by a network, and that cooperate with each other when performing data access and data capture tasks.

Within a distributed database system these things are being distributed:

1 Data

2 Processing logic (e.g., a T-SQL transaction)

3 Control of the execution of the distributed processing logic.

To view distributed databases as simply a means to distribute data is to miss the primary issues of distributing processing logic and the control of their execution. These last two issues are the major technical concerns of distributed databases. These issues are very problematic within production environments, particularly when you attempt to update distributed data in a manner that avoids update anomalies, or when you attempt to recover a federation of autonomous distributed database systems.

The manner in which a distributed database system is implemented is based upon its system architecture. The architecture of a computing system is nothing more than a set of enumerated design principles, standards, definitions, and rules which, when taken together, serve to direct the selection, or creation, of products that are brought together to create a computing system. Applying a system architecture is a process that involves:

1 Identifying the components of a system
2 Specifying the function(s) of each component
3 Defining the interrelationships and interactions among these components in accordance with the system architecture

Architectures of distributed computing systems, in general, are classified with respect to these criteria:

1 Degree of coupling
2 How they are interconnected
3 Degree of interdependence
4 Mode of synchronization

When viewed according to these criteria, the SYBASE Replication Server can be classified as a loosely coupled, point-to-point, semi-autonomous, asynchronous data distribution system.

Introduction to the SYBASE Replication Server

The SYBASE Replication Server (RS) is an asynchronous mechanism that supports the continuous replication and distribution of subscribed transactions. Because T-SQL transactions involving the modification of "text" and "image" data types are treated differently (than the other data types) within the Sybase SQL Server 4.9.2 database transaction log, T-SQL transactions involving "text" and "image" data types are not presently supported by the Replication Server.
1. To receive a replicated transaction, a target site subscribes to published data.

For transactions to be replicated and distributed:

1 The primary table(s), that a transaction modifies, must be published at their source.
2 The subscribed rows within the published primary tables must be loaded into their replicate tables (i.e., the target site).

3. Whenever a transaction modifies subscribed rows, the transaction (that is, the log record; within the log records are the "before" and/or "after" image of each table row the transaction modifies) is delivered and applied to all replicate tables that have a subscription to the published primary table.
4. If the target becomes unavailable, the transactions are stored until the connection to the target is re-established. When the target comes back online, the transactions are automatically forwarded to the target.

The important point to grasp here is that it is really a subscribed transaction, not simply data, that is being replicated and distributed by the Replication Server.

Alternative techniques for distributing data and transactions using SYBASE

Overall, SYBASE supports a limited number of techniques for distributing data. These are the data distribution techniques presently supported by SYBASE:

1. Table Bulk Unload, Transfer, and Load
2. Database Dump, Transfer, and Load
3. Transaction Log Dump, Transfer, and Load
4. Trigger-based Model
5. Table Snapshot
6. Two-Phase Commit Protocol
7. SYBASE Replication Server

Each of these alternatives will be described, and their limitations will be presented. For items 1 through 3, it is assumed that table rows in the source database are not being continually modified.

One technique the SYBASE Replication Server does not support is "update anywhere." At minimum, in order to maintain data integrity, the "update anywhere" technique depends upon some mechanism that is capable of synchronizing transactions across all participating SQL Servers. The SYBASE Replication Server does not have a mechanism that synchronizes transactions across multiple SQL Servers; however, the Two-Phase Commit protocol that supports "update anywhere" is provided by SYBASE SQL Servers. Exploring the "update anywhere" technique in detail is not appropriate within this book as it is one technique that the SYBASE Replication Server does not support.

A comparison and contrast of these techniques will not be undertaken. Nor will a guideline be provided to enable you to select when to use one technique versus another. As long as they satisfy your business requirements, each of these techniques is a valid approach to data distribution. The suitability of one technique versus another is always relative to your particular situation.

Table bulk unload, transfer, and load

Table Bulk Load Transfer is one of the oldest techniques for distributing data. SYBASE provides the bcp utility to support loading and unloading individual tables in bulk. This asynchronous technique works like this:

1. On a per-table basis, use bcp to unload the data into a file.
2. Transfer the bulk data file to the target site. Transfer can be accomplished via file transfer across the network or by manually shipping media, such as tapes.
3. At the target site, on a per table basis, use bcp to load the data into the replicate table.

Typically, table bulk load transfer is not a continuous process; it is a batch process. This batch process may be automated, manual, or a combination of both approaches.

While bulk load transfer is a time-proven technique, it has these limitations:

1. Transactional consistency is not guaranteed.
2. Transactions against the primary tables must be stopped during the unload step.
3. Has a long latency period.
4. Your existing network may not be able to handle the additional load of transferring the files.
5. The target site is read-only.

If the primary database contains corrupt data, then the target database will also contain the corrupted data.

Database dump, transfer, and load

To support the Database Dump, Transfer and Load technique, SYBASE provides the dump database and load database utilities. This asynchronous technique works like this:

1. Use the dump database utility to dump a SYBASE database. When you dump a SYBASE database the entire contents of the database, as well as all completed transactions, are written to a file on a device or to a tape.
2. Transfer the dump file to the target site. Transfer can be accomplished via file transfer across the network or by manually shipping media, such as tapes.

3 Use the load database utility to load the file (created by the dump database utility) into the target database.

Typically, this technique is not a continuous process; it is a batch process. This batch process may be automated, manual, or a combination of both approaches.

While this is another time-proven technique, it has these limitations:

1. Locking, disk I/O, and CPU resource utilization are high.
2. Has a long latency period.
3. Your existing network may not be able to handle the additional load of transferring the files.
4. The target site is read-only.
5. You cannot continue to read the replicate data while the target database is being loaded.
6. If the primary database contains corrupt data, then the target database will also contain the corrupted data.

Transaction Log dump, transfer, and load

To support the Transaction Log Dump, Transfer and Load technique, SYBASE provides the dump transaction and load transaction utilities. This asynchronous technique works like this:

1. Use the dump transaction utility to dump a SYBASE database transaction log. When you dump a SYBASE database transaction log, log records created since the last database or transaction log dump are written to a file on a device or to a tape. Once the transaction log has been dumped, the inactive portion of the transaction log is truncated.
2. Transfer the dump file to the target site. Transfer can be accomplished via file transfer across the network or by manually shipping media, such as tapes.
3. Use the load transaction utility to load the file (created by the dump transaction utility) into the target database.

Typically, this technique is not a continuous process, it is a batch process. This batch process may be automated, manual, or a combination of both approaches.

While this is another time-proven technique, it has these limitations:

1. Locking, disk I/O, and CPU resource utilization are high.
2. It has a long latency period.
3. Your existing network may not be able to handle the additional load of transferring the files.
4. You cannot continue to read the replicate data while the log is being loaded.

5. Transactions against the primary tables must be stopped during the dump step.
6. If the primary log contains corrupted log records, then the target log will also contain corrupted log records.

Trigger-based model

SYBASE triggers are a special type of stored procedure that compares the results of an "insert," "update," or "delete" transaction against a table, or column, and then takes some subsequent action.

With a trigger-based model, the consumer assembles their own replication-specific application using triggers. Whenever a change is made to the source data, that change activates replication-specific code inside the source database (that is, a trigger fires) which begins the replication process (that is, some subsequent software executes).

Trigger-based model limitations include:

1. Triggers simply transfer individual data items that have been modified.
2. In and of themselves, triggers do not keep track of transactions.
3. Triggers allow one-way replication only.
4. Data at a replicate site is read-only and should not be modified.
5. The execution of triggers within a database imposes a performance overhead to that database.
6. Triggers require careful management by database administrators. Someone needs to keep track of all the "triggers" going off when data is modified.
7. The activation of triggers in a database cannot be easily "rolled back" or undone at the source site, and cannot be undone at the target site(s).
8. The replication system is closely tied to the operations of the source database (i.e., code must be executed within the source database while the transaction itself executes).
9. It places too many demands for coordination between application developers and system administrators.
10. The complex web of triggers, tables, stored procedures, application code, and system administration tasks may be too difficult to maintain for a large application.
11. Conflict resolution demands arising from system component failures will likely be extreme and involve elaborate reconciliation heuristics.

12 As the variety of data subsets (that need to be replicated) increases, the degree of complexity of this approach increases radically.
13 It is entirely up to the customer to build the application that keeps track of, and protects the integrity of, transactions (even including those related to system component failures).

Table snapshot

A snapshot is a copy of the contents of an individual table, of subsets of tables, or collections of tables. The consumer assembles their own replication-specific application using T-SQL (often nested within 4GL and/or 3GL languages). This application code then supports the asynchronous, or synchronous, distribution of the snapshots.

Table snapshots have these limitations:

1 They copy the contents of data tables without maintaining the atomicity of a transaction. With transactions broken, the integrity of the distributed data is up for grabs (i.e., threatened).
2 They provide only a one-way path for data. While data can be copied to multiple locations, the copies are read-only and no changes can be made to the distributed data.

Atomicity is one of the five ACIDS characteristics of data distribution:

Atomicity	The entire sequence of actions must be either completed or aborted, i.e., it cannot be partially successful.
Consistency	A transaction takes the local computing system and its resources from one consistent state to another.
Isolation	A local transaction's effect is not visible to other local transactions until the transaction is committed.
Durability	Changes made by the committed transactions are permanent and should tolerate system failure.
Serializability	As a local transaction in progress depends on certain local information, this local information is locked to prevent any other transaction from changing it.

If the infrastructure components (such as the SYBASE Replication Server) cannot supply ACIDS characteristics, then processes must do so. Additional precautions must be taken if the ability to support ACIDS across multiple database servers is required.

Table snapshot application code can incorporate the Two-Phase Commit Protocol, and thereby become a synchronous distribution technique.

Two-Phase Commit protocol

The Two-Phase Commit (2-PC) protocol is an elaborate handshake mechanism, across a network, that allows distributed sites to coordinate their acceptance of a transaction. SYBASE supports a 2-PC Protocol between distributed SQL Servers. SYBASE accomplishes this through the Open Client library. In addition, the SQL Server itself provides automatic 2-PC protocol for databases that are managed by the same SQL Server process.

As the name implies, the protocol is composed of two phases: the first phase ensures that all modification transactions are processed and then instructs the participants to prepare to commit the transaction, while the second phase instructs all participants to commit, or roll back, the transaction.

A Two-Phase Commit Protocol transaction will succeed if, and only if, all interconnected distributed sites agree to it. All distributed sites need to synchronously approve a transaction before it is accepted. If any one site is unavailable, the transaction will have to wait (i.e., it will hang)—this exposure to business operations may be unacceptable. Another unfortunate side-effect of this technique is that the protocol produces a lot of messages that go back and forth between sites as they coordinate the acceptance of the data. This message passing overhead puts a significant burden on the network. However, by using this technique it is possible to maintain (in a timely fashion) the integrity of the distributed data.

Once again, the consumer implements this technique through application code. Programmatic solutions must be provided by the consumer to handle all possible failure scenarios, such as when a participating site crashes between the first and second phases.

SYBASE Replication Server

The SYBASE Replication Server product is an event-driven and transaction-based mechanism that provides consistent and reliable delivery of transactions or data. In order to receive a replicated transaction, a target site subscribes to published data.

While programmatic solutions are not required to replicate transactions, the consumer must implement replication language constructs, establish routes, and train their operations staff on how to administer a federation of semi-autonomous databases.

The SYBASE Replication Server has these limitations:

1 Provides read-only copies.
2 Prohibits the direct updating of replicant copies.
3 Recovering from system component failures involves very complex recovery heuristics.
4 As the system architecture ensures a period of latency, the literal data values of the copies are not current with the literal data values of the primary data source.
5 There is a possibility of lost transactions as a result of system component failure.

All of these limitations, as well as the concepts of subscribing and publishing data, will be discussed in depth in later chapters.

Brief overview of the major replication system components

The basic replication system is made up of the following major components:

1 SQL Server(s)—These manage the databases containing primary or replicated data.
2 Log Transfer Manager(s) (LTM)—An Open Server/Open Client application that monitors a SQL Server's transaction log, and detects changes to a primary SQL Server database and passes those changes onto a Replication Server process.
3 Replication Server(s)—A multithreaded Open Server/Open Client application that maintains replicated data at multiple sites on a network and processes data transactions received from other Replication Servers on the network. In addition, the Replication Server distributes replication and subscription information to other Replication Servers.

Within UNIX environments, SQL Servers, Log Transfer Managers, and Replication Servers execute as heavyweight processes under the control of the operating system.

This design of a basic replication system is represented in Fig. 1-1.

In the following chapters, I will investigate the SYBASE Replication Server product by studying the structure and features of its individual components and subcomponents and by analyzing their behavior.

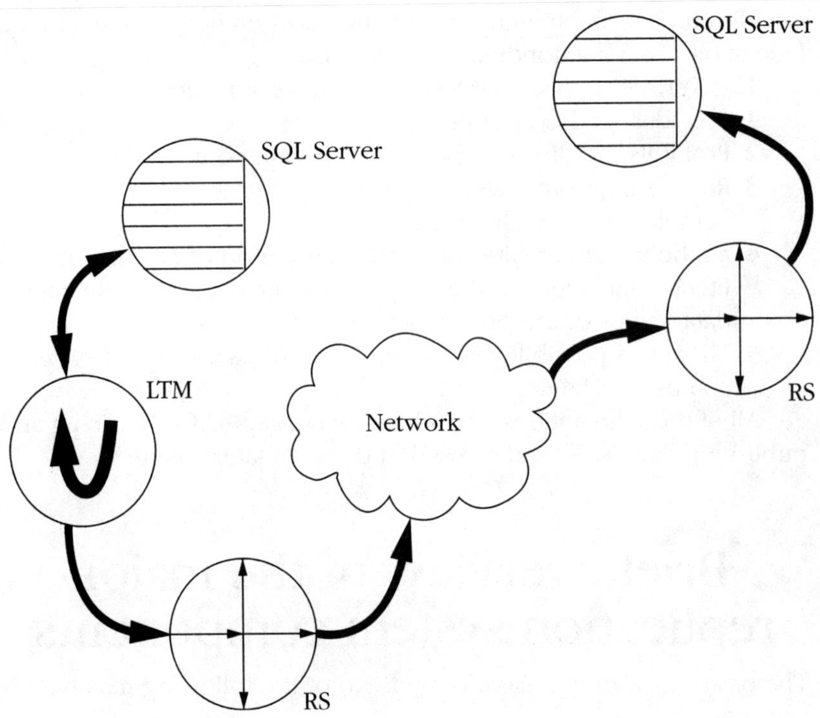

1-1 *Design of a basic Replication Server*

2

Replication Server

The Replication Server is a multithreaded Open Server/Open Client-based application that maintains replicated data at multiple sites on a network and processes data transactions received from other Replication Servers on the network. In addition, the Replication Server distributes replication and subscription information to other Replication Servers.

The SYBASE Open Server product is a library of utility routines that enable the consumer to build his or her own application servers. The SYBASE Open Client product is a library of utility routines that enable the consumer to build his or her own client applications. Within client/server application architectures, the client makes requests of the server and the server provides responses to these requests. When you combine these products, you create a gateway. A gateway acts as a communication intermediary between client and server applications, and between other gateways applications.

A multithreaded application contains a suite of executable threads. Each thread is capable of undertaking a variety of routines, each of which are designed to accomplish specific tasks. Threads often share access to common computing resources, such as memory and disk drives, allocated by the operating system to the application. While the Replication Server is a multithreaded heavyweight process, the product consumer does not have the capability of controlling the manner in which the Replication Server schedules thread processing.

Design of the Replication Server

The Replication Server contains multiple threads, daemons, and internal libraries. The key to understanding the SYBASE Replication Server is through gaining an appreciation for these threads, daemons, and libraries:

- Log Transfer Manager USER (Executor)
- Stable Queue Manager
- Stable Queue Transaction Interface
- Distributor
- Replication Server Interface
- Data Server Interface
- Replication Server USER
- Replication Server Interface USER
- USER
- dAIO
- dALARM
- dCM
- dSUB
- Subscription Resolution Engine
- Message Delivery Module
- Transaction Delivery Module

Each of these components of the Replication Server will be described, an explanation of how they work will be given, and examples of how they interoperate with each other will be provided. Regrettably, due to the fact that these internal components function in a mutually interdependent manner, it is not possible to introduce them in a linear sequential manner wherein each is fully defined when it is first introduced to the reader. Therefore, it is recommended that you refer to the glossary whenever you encounter a term with which you are not familiar.

Log Transfer Manager USER (Executor) thread

The Executor is a Log Transfer Manager Open Client connection to the Replication Server. A Replication Server can handle multiple concurrent Executor threads. There will be one Executor thread for each Log Transfer Manager-to-Replication Server connection.

The Executor has two main tasks:

1. Verifies that Log Transfer Manager submissions are normalized.
2. Writes the Log Transfer Manager submissions onto a dedicated stable queue. A stable queue is used by the Replication Server to spool messages. Messages reside among these suites of stable queues until they are delivered to a remote Replication Server by a Replication Server Interface thread, or until they are delivered to a SQL Server by a Data

Server Interface thread. Stable queues are located on partitions. A partition is a physical device name used by the Replication Server.

The Executor thread first verifies that Log Transfer Manager submissions are normalized. It does this by checking columns, converting data types and reordering columns to match the column order in the replication definition. A replication definition is a formal description of a source SQL Server database table, whose data you want to be replicated to one or more destination SQL Server database tables. Once the columns are checked, the Log Transfer Manager submission is considered to be normalized. As the normalization process takes longer if the column order in the replication definition differs from the column order in the physical database, you can avoid degrading Replication Server performance by ensuring that a replication definition is implemented in a fully normalized manner.

Following normalization, the Executor writes, via its dedicated Stable Queue Manager thread, the parsed and normalized Log Transfer Manager submissions onto a dedicated inbound stable queue. For a graphical representation of the Executor Thread, refer to Fig. 2-1 below.

While each Executor has its own dedicated Stable Queue Manager to work with, the Executor's dedicated Stable Queue Manager will still exist within the Replication Server even if the Executor thread goes down. However, if the Log Transfer Manager-to-Replication Server connection breaks because a Log Transfer Manager is no longer running (that is, the Log Transfer Manager crashes or it is shut down in a controlled manner), both the Executor and its dedicated Stable Queue Manager threads will die.

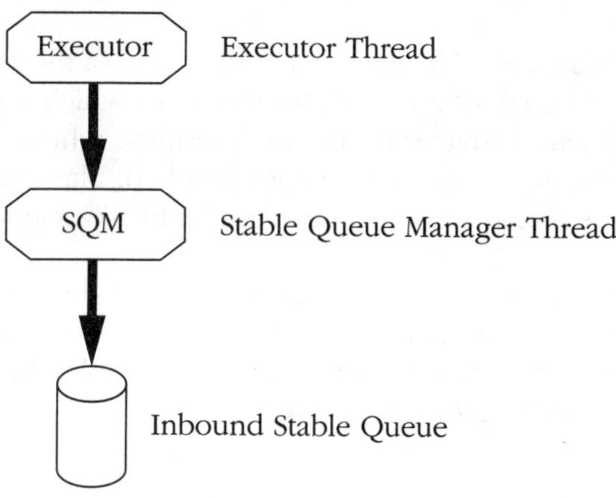

2-1 *Executor thread*

Stable Queue Manager thread

The Stable Queue Manager thread manages access to, and the organization of, a given stable queue (on a given stable device). The Stable Queue Manager is responsible for:

1 Reclaiming space in outbound stable queues after transactions have been forwarded.
2 Reclaiming space in inbound stable queues when a transaction has been rolled back.

While reclaiming space in outbound stable queues, the Stable Queue Manager is constrained by the *save interval* Replication Server configuration parameter. The purpose of this user-controlled configuration parameter is to ensure that outbound transactions are not purged prematurely, thereby facilitating the recovery of a crashed replication system.

Stable Queue Manager threads are started when the Replication Server boots (that is, when it starts up). There is one dedicated Stable Queue Manager for each stable queue that must be accessed by the Replication Server. This is the case whether an inbound, an outbound, or a materialization-type stable queue is being accessed by the Replication Server.

The Stable Queue Manager cooperates with the Distributor thread and Stable Queue Transaction Interface thread for a stable queue. There will always be one Stable Queue Manager thread for each Log Transfer Manager-to-Replication Server connection, one Stable Queue Manager thread for each target site Replication Server, and one Stable Queue Manager thread for each target replicant database. On behalf of the Executor to which it is dedicated, a Stable Queue Manager places Log Transfer Manager submissions on an inbound stable queue.

Each Stable Queue Manager can write to any of the outbound stable queues on behalf of a Distributor thread to which it is dedicated. The Stable Queue Manager is able to determine which stable queue to write to by how the stable queue is identified. The identity (that is, name) of the stable queue includes the identity, or name, of the target database.

In addition, a Stable Queue Manager is used during subscription materialization to write materialization data to materialization stable queues. For a graphical representation of the Stable Queue Manager Thread, refer to Fig. 2-2 on next page.

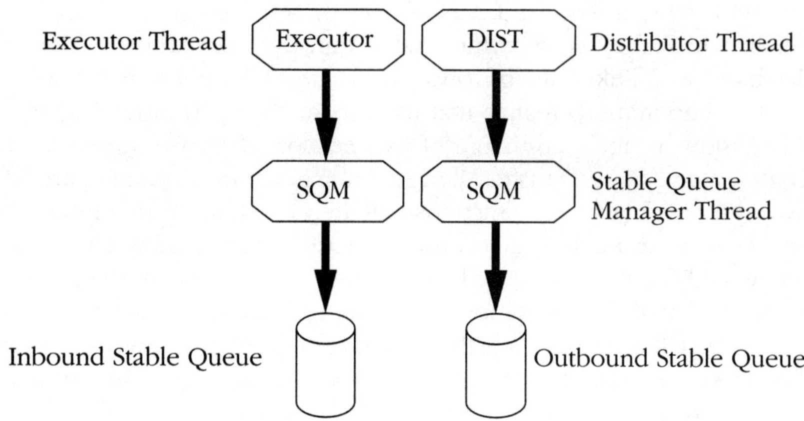

2-2 *Stable Queue Manager thread*

Stable Queue Transaction Interface thread

Any Replication Server thread that reads from a stable queue does so via its own dedicated Stable Queue Transaction Interface thread. The Stable Queue Transaction Interface thread monitors and orders transactions that reach the Replication Server. Like Stable Queue Manager threads, Stable Queue Transaction Interface threads are started when the Replication Server boots. The Replication Server will start one dedicated Stable Queue Transaction Interface thread for each inbound stable queue and will start one dedicated Stable Queue Transaction Interface thread for each outbound stable queue.

A Stable Queue Transaction Interface thread has a volatile memory cache, called a transaction cache, where it stores Log Transfer Manager submissions it is currently processing. The size of this transaction cache is a tunable Replication Server parameter (sqt_max_cache_size). To enable recovery from catastrophic system failures, it is possible to dump the contents of this cache. However, dumping the contents of the cache introduces the loss of transaction integrity. Whenever this occurs, the product consumer must provide the programmatic solution to this loss of transaction integrity.

On behalf of a given Distributor thread, a dedicated Stable Queue Transaction Interface thread reads a stream of messages from a given inbound stable queue, and reassembles these transactions (in the order in which they were committed within their primary SQL Server database) as a linked list of rows (transaction IDs) per transaction.

It is important to realize that the stream of Log Transfer Manager submissions is likely a mixture of two or more database transactions. That is, a given Log Transfer Manager submission may contain parts of two or more database transactions that are mixed one with another. If you were to examine log records of the SQL Server transaction log, you would see that log records themselves contain a mixture of statements for multiple transactions. The Stable Queue Transaction Interface thread has to separate this mixture of database transactions. It then has to reassemble these statements into there original logical unit of work. To accomplish this task, the Stable Queue Transaction Interface thread follows a first-in-first-out (FIFO) method in its processing of Log Transfer Manager submissions. The Stable Queue Transaction Interface thread will pick up the first transaction statement within the Log Transfer Manager submission. Each transaction statement has associated with it the identity of the logical unit of work it is associated with. The Stable Queue Transaction Interface thread will continue to pick up transaction statement, but it will set aside transaction statements for other transactions, while it works at assembling the logical unit of work it is currently focused upon. The Stable Queue Transaction Interface thread follows this FIFO processing until it encounters the "commit" statement, or the "rollback" statement for this transaction.

When the end of logical unit of work is detected, the Stable Queue Transaction Interface thread sends these reassembled inbound transactions on to the Distributor thread. If a rollback occurs, Stable Queue Transaction Interface thread tells the Stable Queue Manager to delete affected transactions from the inbound stable queue. If a Log Transfer Manager crashes within a state where its most recent Log Transfer Manager submission lacks an end of transaction statement, the Stable Queue Transaction Interface thread will hang in the middle of its FIFO processing. If this happens, the integrity of the transaction the Stable Queue Transaction Interface thread is working on is lost. In addition, the integrity of any subsequent transaction mixed within the recent Log Transfer Manager submission is lost as well. There is no means provided by SYBASE to recover from this loss of transaction integrity. It is up to the consumer to provide a programmatic solution to this window of vulnerability.

Stable Queue Transaction Interface threads also provide support to Data Server Interface threads. On behalf of a Data Server Interface thread, a Stable Queue Transaction Interface thread reads transactions from a given outbound stable queue and passes on to the Data Server

Interface thread a linked list of rows (transaction IDs) per transaction. If the Data Server Interface thread goes down while it is pulling transactions from the outbound stable queue, it will automatically continue where it left off after it has been restarted. A loss of transaction integrity will not occur in this case. However, in order to ensure that the transaction integrity of the target database is not lost, you must ensure that absolutely no other transactions modify the target database while the Data Server Interface thread is down, or while it is being recovered.

For a graphical representation of the Stable Queue Transaction Interface Thread, refer to Fig. 2-3 below.

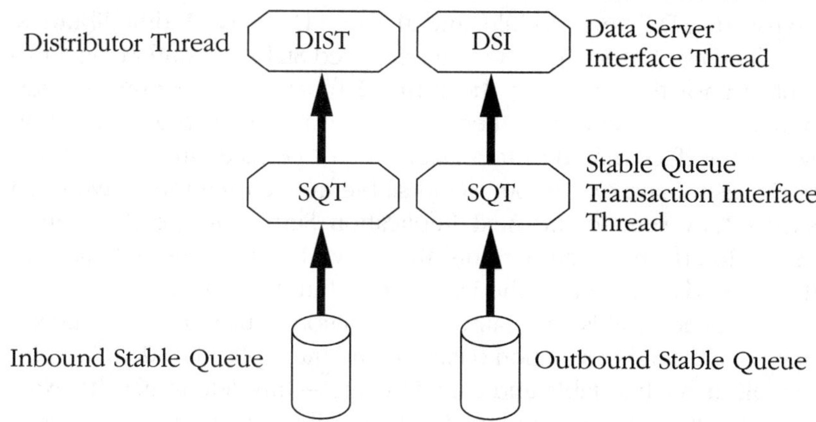

2-3 *Stable Queue Transaction Interface thread*

Distributor thread

A Distributor thread exists for each database under the control of a given Replication Server. At boot time the Replication Server starts up each of its Distributor threads, and sets up each inbound stable queues that supports a given Distributor thread. The purpose of the Distributor thread is to:

1. Read transactions from a given inbound stable queue, via a dedicated stable queue transaction interface thread.
2. Determine which subscribed transactions a particular data server is interested in.
3. Forward subscribed transactions onto target data servers.

Working with the stable queue transaction interface thread, the distributor thread uses the linked list of transactions (created by the stable queue transaction interface thread) and puts together all rows for a transaction in their commit order.

In order to determine which subscribed transactions a particular data server is interested in, the Distributor thread resolves the tables affected by each transaction statement, and then decides the destination of each transaction statement. It reaches these conclusions by making library calls to:

1 The Subscription Resolution Engine
2 The Transaction Delivery Module
3 The Message Delivery Module

While each Distributor thread has its own dedicated pair of Stable Queue Manager and Stable Queue Transaction Interface threads, all Distributor threads share the same Subscription Resolution Engine, Transaction Delivery Module, and Message Delivery Module libraries.

The Distributor thread uses a dedicated Stable Queue Manager to write transaction rows (in the form of function calls) onto an outbound stable queue, whether that queue is going to a Replication Server Interface thread or to a Data Server Interface thread. The function calls remain on the outbound stable queue until they have been successfully sent to the next Replication Server by the Replication Server Interface thread, or until they have been successfully sent to the target data server by the Data Server Interface thread.

A function call is an instance of a function or user-defined function that contains the destination database and the replication definition information (such as table and column names—this determines the exact set of function strings), that the function call is for, and the parameters for the data server operation to be performed at the subscribing site.

For a graphical representation of the Distributor Thread, refer to Fig. 2-4 below.

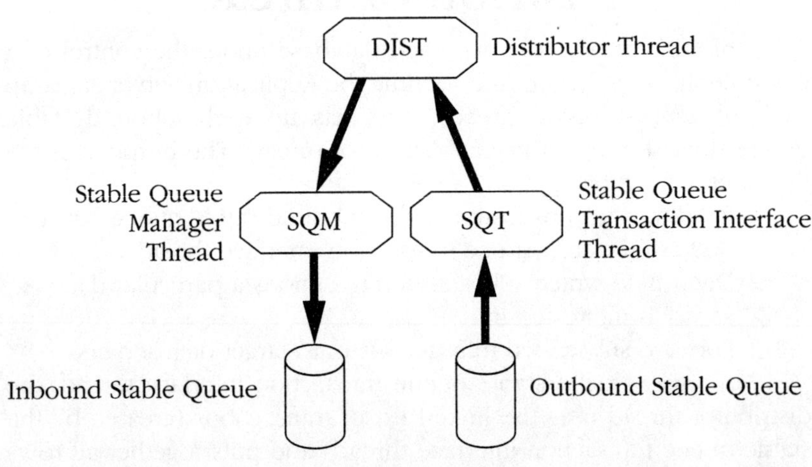

2-4 *Distributor thread*

Subscription Resolution Engine

The Subscription Resolution Engine matches transaction rows with replication subscriptions, using (in memory) Replication Server System Database contents. These in memory Replication Server System Database contents are provided to the Subscription Resolution Engine by the Distributor thread. The Subscription Resolution Engine:

1. Tells the Distributor thread to discard a row if no replication subscriptions match the transaction statement.
2. Decides what operation to replicate, in order to preserve state consistency.
3. Decides whether subscription migration is, or is not, required.
4. Determines which function call to use on the row when applying it to the replicant database.
5. Attaches the identity, or name, of the destination database to each transaction row that it forwards.

For a graphical representation of the Subscription Resolution Engine, refer to Fig. 2-5 below.

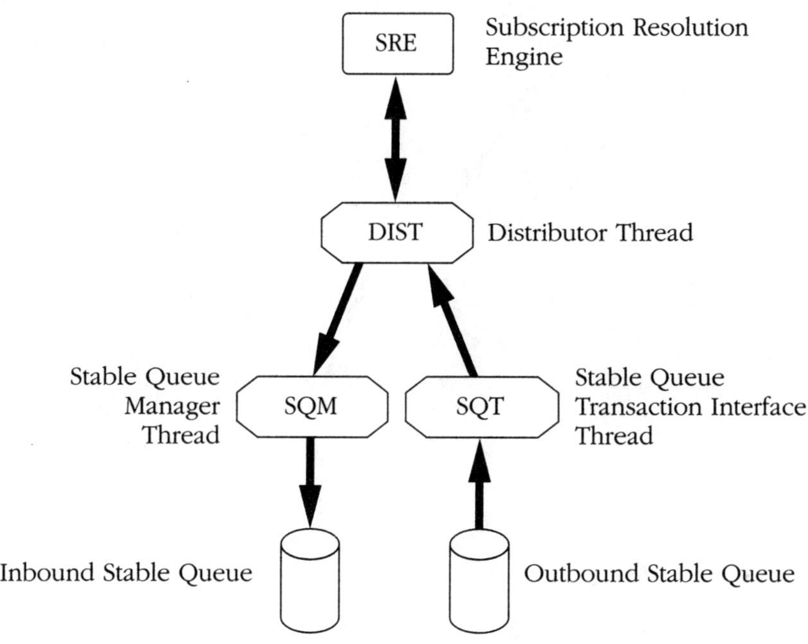

2-5 *Subscription Resolution Engine*

Message Delivery Module

The Message Delivery Module needs information from both the RSSD.rs_routes and the RSSD.rs_repdbs tables. The Message Delivery Module gets this information via the Distributor thread.

When the Message Delivery Module is called by the Distributor thread, it has passed to it the transaction row and the name of the destination Replication Server. Used in memory routing information (contained in the RSSD.rs_routes table), the Message Delivery Module determines the next site that will receive the transaction row. The next site may be either a data server (which the transaction row will reach using a Data Server Interface thread) or a Replication Server (which the transaction row will reach using a Replication Server Interface thread).

The Message Delivery Module adds to the transaction row the destination string of all the next sites. The string of next sites contains all immediate next sites relative to the given Replication Server. That is, the list of next sites does not include any subscribing sites further down a route beyond the next immediate Replication Server.

For a graphical representation of the Message Delivery Module, refer to Fig. 2-6 below.

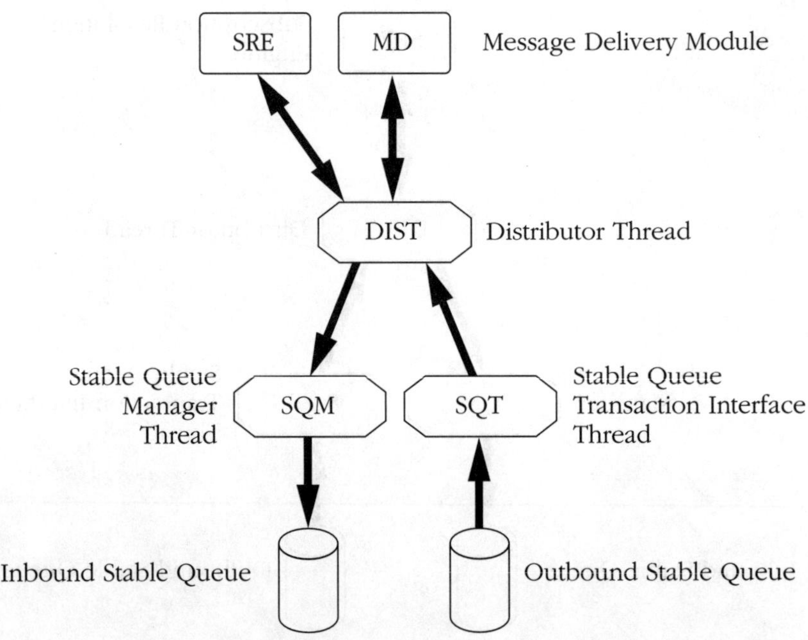

2-6 *Message Delivery Module*

Transaction Delivery Module

The Transaction Delivery Module is called by the Distributor thread to prepare transaction rows to be sent to data servers and other Replication Servers. It is the job of the Transaction Delivery Module to package each transaction row as a function call.

For a graphical representation of the Transaction Delivery Module, refer to Fig. 2-7 below.

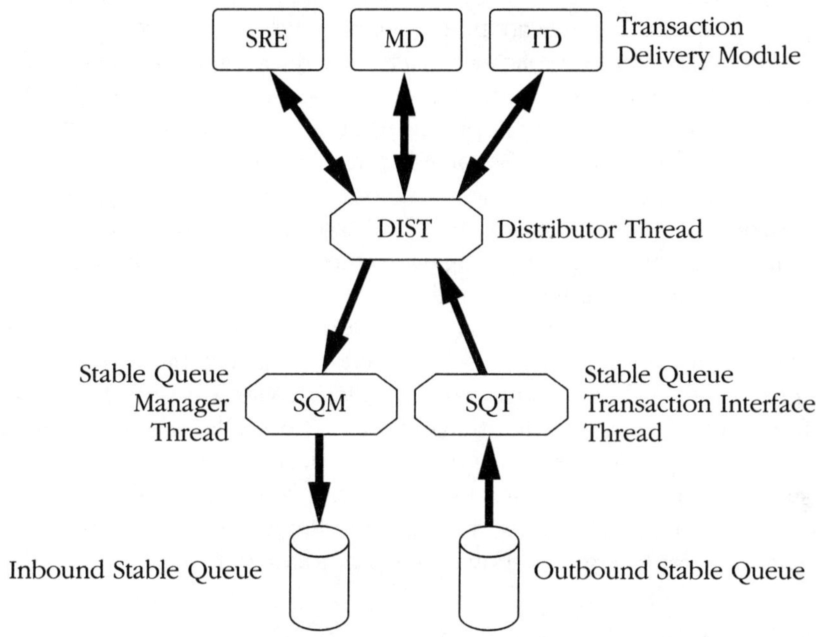

2-7 *Transaction Delivery Module*

Replication Server Interface thread

The Replication Server Interface thread is an asynchronous Open Client connection. A Replication Server uses the RS_RS_user login name and password to establish Open Client connections with another Replication Server. A given Replication Server can support multiple Replication Server Interface threads.

There will be a Replication Server Interface thread for each remote Replication Server that the local Replication Server forwards transactions to. Each Replication Server Interface thread has its own dedicated Stable Queue Manager thread.

All transaction rows (in the form of function calls), written by the dedicated Stable Queue Manager on behalf of a Distributor thread, remain in storage on an outbound stable queue until they are successfully sent to the remote Replication Server by the Replication Server Interface thread. While the Replication Server Interface thread uses an efficient, large packet transfer technique, the size of the transferred packages is a consumer-tunable Replication Server parameter (rsi_packet_size).

The behavior of Replication Server Interface threads is affected by route commands. For example, if the command is given to suspend a particular route, then any Replication Server Interface thread that uses that particular route will become inactive. During the time in which the route is down, outbound stable queues may continue to fill up. When the route is resumed the Replication Server Interface thread will awaken and begin, once again, to transfer function calls to the remote Replication Server reached via the resumed route.

In that a Replication Server can support multiple Log Transfer Manager-to-Replication Server connections, each Replication Server Interface thread must potentially handle a collection of transactions from multiple Log Transfer Managers. Function calls, originating from multiple Log Transfer Managers, may collect on the one outbound stable queue for the destination Replication Server.

For a graphical representation of the Replication Server Interface Thread, refer to Fig. 2-8 shown at top of following page.

Data Server Interface thread

There is one Data Server Interface thread (and accompanying Stable Queue Transaction Interface thread) for each target SQL Server (or Open Server process) a given Replication Server writes to. A given Replication Server can support multiple Data Server Interface threads.

The function of the Data Server Interface thread is to:

1 Read a given outbound Data Server Interface thread stable queue, via a dedicated Stable Queue Transaction Interface thread.

2 As the database maintenance user, apply transactions to the SQL Server that manages the target replicate database.

At boot time, the Replication Server executes the rs_get_lastcommit function when is starts up a Data Server Interface thread. The rs_get_lastcommit function returns all of the rows in the rs_lastcom

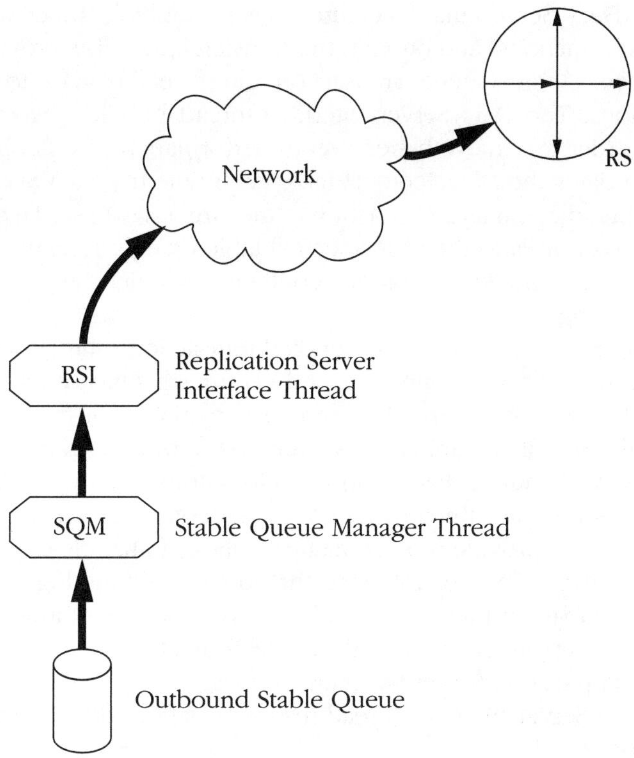

2-8 *Replication Server Interface thread*

mit table. The Replication Server uses this result set to determine the last transaction committed (by the given Data Server Interface thread) from each primary data source of the given target database. You can not be certain that all Data Server Interface threads have been started at boot time, as given target may not be available, such as when the target site has crashed or has run out of available connections.

A Data Server Interface thread will disconnect from the data server, or the Open Server process, whenever that target site crashes. Therefore, during the replication system recovery process, you must keep checking to make sure that all Data Server Interface threads are active, and be prepared to restart Data Server Interface threads as needed.

The Data Server Interface thread maps function strings to the function calls. The Data Server Interface thread determines which function string class to use by establishing the destination of the function call. Determining which particular group of function strings, within a function string class, to use is established by the specific replication definition that is the basis of the function call.

The Data Server Interface thread takes multiple function calls (that is, transactions) and bundles them (using linked lists provided to it from the Stable Queue Transaction Interface thread) into larger transactions. The Data Server Interface thread bundles the transactions in order to achieve better overall performance. The Replication Server updates the rs_lastcommit table each time the Data Server Interface thread commits a transaction in the target database. The Replication Server updates the rs_lastcommit table by executing the stored procedure rs_update_lastcommit contained within the rs_commit function string.

If there is an error with the bundled transactions, the Data Server Interface thread will unbundle it and send each function call separately. The Data Server Interface thread does this error handling automatically, and in a manner transparent to the product consumer. To address error handling that is outside of its automated capabilities, the Data Server Interface thread writes to an exceptions log. The product consumer must provide programmatic solutions to handle errors written into the Data Server Interface thread's exceptions log. Just because a Data Server Interface thread is active, you cannot assume that there are no errors that you must handle yourself.

Like Replication Server Interface threads:

1 Data Server Interface thread results are affected by connection commands.

2 The Data Server Interface thread must also be able to handle a collection of transactions that collect on the one outbound Data Server Interface thread stable queue of the target SQL Server.

For a graphical representation of the Data Server Interface Thread, refer to Fig. 2-9 at top of following page.

Replication Server USER thread

The Replication Server USER thread is an Open Client connection to the Replication Server. The sole purpose of this thread is to create or drop replication subscriptions at the primary Replication Server.

Replication Server Interface USER thread

The Replication Server Interface USER thread is an Open Client connection to the Replication Server. This thread is used to handle messages coming from a remote Replication Server to this Replication Server.

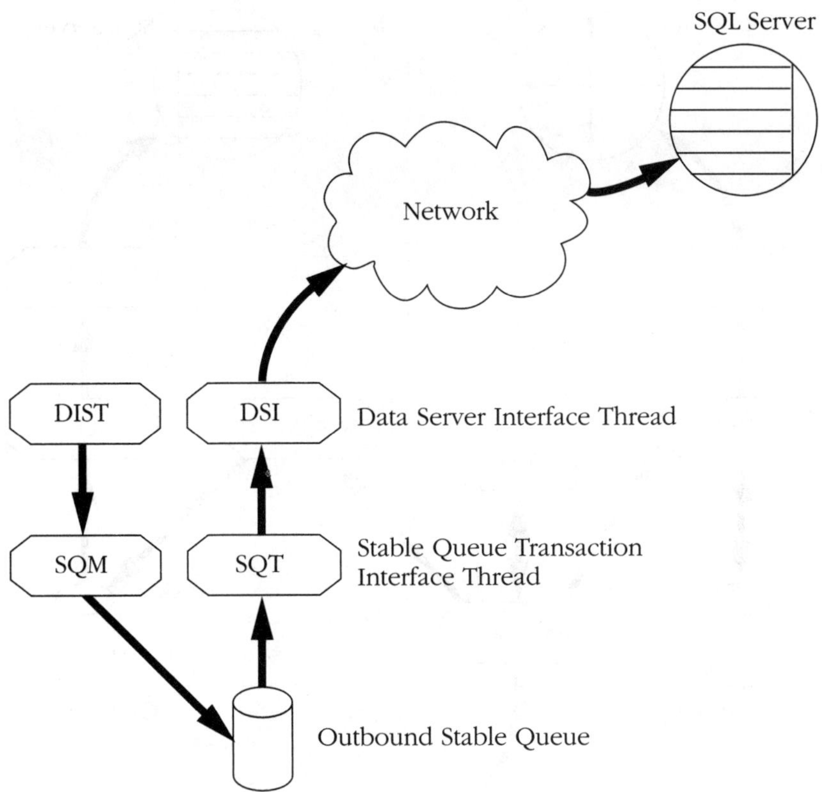

2-9 *Data Server Interface thread*

The Replication Server Interface USER thread calls the Message Delivery Module to decide where to send a given message. If the message is for a SQL Server that the Replication Server supports, then the message is written to a Data Server Interface thread outbound stable queue. If the message is destined for another Replication Server, then it is written to a Replication Server Interface thread outbound stable queue.

For a graphical representation of the Replication Server Interface USER thread, refer to Fig. 2-10 at top of following page.

USER thread

The USER thread manages an Open Client login connection from a Replication Server user, typically the Replication Server administrator.

Replication Server daemons

Within UNIX environments, daemon processes are processes that do not have a terminal or login shell associated with them. As such, dae-

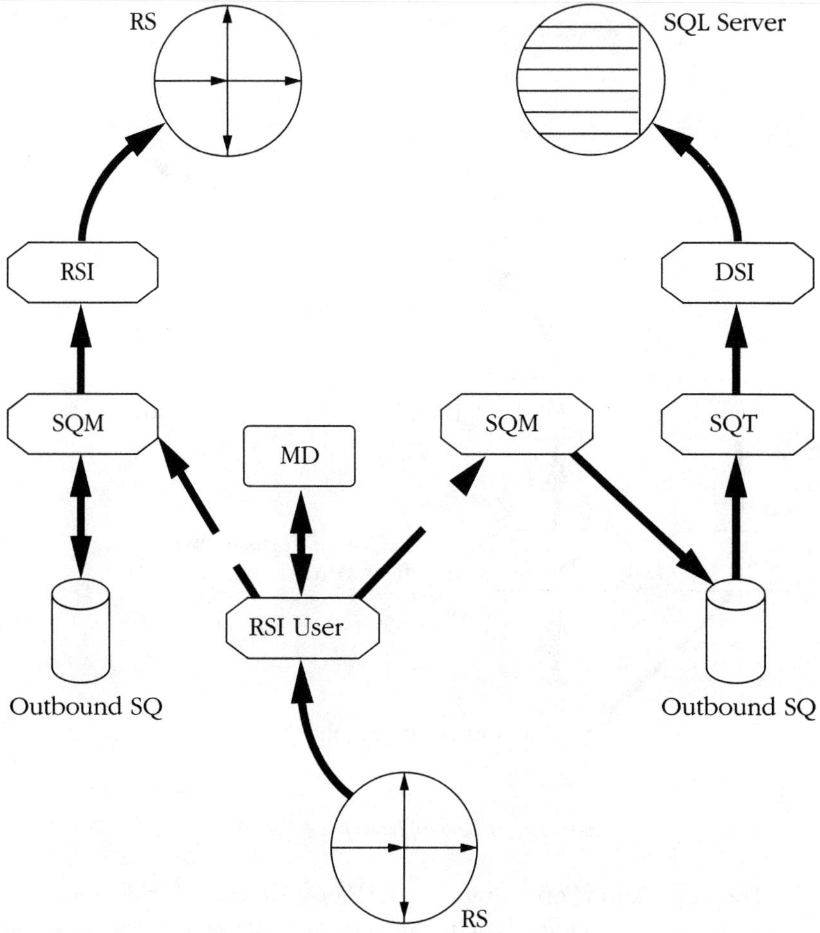

2-10 *Replication Server Interface USER thread*

mon processes execute in the background waiting to receive instructions from another process, or to undertake periodic tasks. The Replication Server has these four daemon processes:

1. dAIO—Manages asynchronous I/O operations to stable queues for the Replication Server.
2. dALARM—Keeps track of alarms set by other threads.
3. dCM—Manages connections to SQL Servers, to another Replication Server, and to Open Server programs.
4. dSUB—Sleeps for a period of time (a configurable quantum), then wakes up to attempt to restart any subscriptions that have failed.

Replication Server internals—messages from a Log Transfer Manager

The Replication Server works in the following manner when interacting with a Log Transfer Manager:

1. The Executor thread verifies that the Log Transfer Manager submission is normalized, i.e., it checks columns, converts datatypes, and reorders columns to match the column order in the replication definition. Because the Replication Server reorders columns to match the column order in the replication definition, performance suffers when the order of columns in the replication definition(s) do not match the order of the columns within the corresponding table.
2. Via its dedicated Stable Queue Manager thread, the Executor writes the parsed, and normalized, Log Transfer Manager submissions onto a dedicated inbound stable queue.
3. The dedicated Stable Queue Transaction Interface thread reads a stream of messages from the inbound stable queue.
4. Within its dedicated in memory transaction cache, the Stable Queue Transaction Interface thread reassembles these transactions into the order in which they were committed within their primary SQL Server database, as a linked list of rows (transaction IDs) per transaction. If a rollback occurs, Stable Queue Transaction Interface thread tells the Stable Queue Manager to delete affected transactions from the inbound stable queue.
5. The Stable Queue Transaction Interface thread writes, via the Stable Queue Manager thread, the reassembled transactions into a transaction cache stable queue.
6. When the end of transaction is detected, the Stable Queue Transaction Interface thread passes these inbound linked lists of rows onto the Distributor thread.
7. Via a dedicated Stable Queue Transaction Interface thread, the Distributor thread reads transactions from the transaction cache stable queue.
8. The Distributor thread uses the linked list created by the Stable Queue Transaction Interface thread to put all rows for a transaction together, and to put the transactions themselves in commit order.

8.1 A library call to the Subscription Resolution Engine is made by the Distributor thread in order to match transaction rows with subscriptions (using in-memory RSSD contents, which it actually gets through the Distributor thread). The Subscription Resolution Engine tells the Distributor thread to discard a row if no subscriptions match.

8.1.1 The Subscription Resolution Engine determines if subscription migration is required.

8.1.2 The Subscription Resolution Engine determines which function call to use on the transaction row when applying it to the replicant database. A function call is an instance of a function, or user-defined function (UDF), that contains the destination database and the replication definition information (such as table and column names—this determines the exact set of function strings), that the function call is for, and the parameters for the data server operation to be performed at the subscribing site.

8.1.3 The Subscription Resolution Engine attaches the ID of the destination database to each transaction row.

8.2 The Distributor thread makes a library call to the Message Delivery Module and passes to it the transaction row (along with its destination ID).

8.2.1 The Message Delivery uses in-memory routing information (in the RSSD) to determine the next site, either to a data server or an Replication Server.

8.2.2 The Message Delivery adds to the transaction row a destination string of all the next sites.

8.3 The Transaction Delivery Module is called by the Distributor thread to prepare transaction rows.

8.3.1 The Transaction Delivery Module packages these transactions rows as function calls to be sent to data servers and other Replication Servers.

9 The Distributor thread uses a dedicated Stable Queue Manager to write the packaged transaction rows, in the form of function calls, onto the appropriate outbound stable queue.

Replication Server internals—messages to an SQL Server

The Replication Server works in the following manner when interacting with a SQL Server:

1 On behalf of a Data Server Interface thread, a monitoring Stable Queue Transaction Interface thread reads messages (in the form of packaged function calls) from the outbound Data Server Interface thread stable queue and passes them on to the Data Server Interface thread as a linked list.

2 The Data Server Interface thread maps function strings to the function calls on the linked list.

3 The Data Server Interface thread takes multiple function strings and bundles them into larger transactions.

- **3.1** If there is an error with the bundled transactions, the Data Server Interface thread will unbundle it and send each component transaction separately; it does this automatically and transparently.
  - **3.1.1** The Data Server Interface thread only writes to the exceptions log when there is an error with the transaction, and the error action calls for it.

4 As the Replicant Database (RDB) maintenance user, DB_Maint_user, the Data Server Interface thread applies transactions to a data server (i.e., to any Open Server based program).

- **4.1** In the case of Remote Procedure Call (RPC) type transactions, errors in specifying output template parameters will manifest at this point as the Replication Server tries to apply the transactions using invalid function strings.
  - **4.1.1** The Data Server Interface thread will go down as a result of encountering this type of error.

Replication Server internals—messages to another Replication Server

The Replication Server works in the following manner when forwarding transactions to another Replication Server:

1 On behalf of a Replication Server Interface thread, a monitoring Stable Queue Transaction Interface thread reads messages (in the form of packaged function calls) from the outbound Replication Server Interface thread stable queue and passes them on to the Replication Server Interface thread as a linked list.
2 Using the RS_RS_user login name and password, the Replication Server Interface thread forwards the packaged function calls to the Replicant Replication Server.

Replication Server internals—messages from another Replication Server

The Replication Server works in the following manner when receiving transactions from another Replication Server:

1 When messages, in the form of function calls, arrive on the inbound stable queue, the monitoring Stable Queue Transaction Interface thread passes the messages onto the Replication Server Interface USER thread.
2 The Replication Server Interface USER thread makes a call to the Message Delivery Module to decide where to send a given message.
3 The Message Delivery uses in-memory routing information in the RSSD to determine the next site, either to a data server or Replication Server.
4 The Replication Server Interface USER thread uses a dedicated Stable Queue Manager to write the function calls onto an outbound Data Server Interface thread stable queue or an outbound Replication Server Interface thread stable queue.

Generating a Replication Server

The rs_install utility is used to generate a Replication Server. The rs_install utility takes an installation parameter file as input, as follows:

```
$SYBASE/install/rs_install < installation_parameter_filename
```

Before you start to generate a Replication Server, make certain that:

1 You have loaded the SYBASE Replication Server software from the distribution media provided to you by the vendor.
2 All SQL Servers used to store primary data are at version 4.92, or later, and are at the Emergency Bug Fix (EBF) level indicated in your SYBASE Replication Server Release Bulletin.

3 The SYBASE environment variable (on the host computer on which you have loaded the SYBASE Replication Server software) is set to the correct SYBASE directory.

A Replication Server's installation parameter file must contain:

1 The globally unique name of the Replication Server. Each Replication Server name must be unique within the Replication system.
2 A Boolean variable that indicates whether the Replication Server will manage SQL Server databases with primary data, may submit asynchronous transactions, and/or may serve as an intermediate site in an indirect route. Alternatively, the Replication Server will merely manage SQL Server databases with primary data.
3 The full path name of the first raw disk partition (that is at least 20MB in size) for the Replication Server's stable queue(s). Additional raw disk partitions can be added to the Replication Server after the Replication Server is installed.
4 A logical identifier name for the first raw disk partition.
5 The size, in megabytes, of the first raw disk partition.
6 The Replication Server login name that other Replication Servers will use to connect to this particular Replication Server.
7 The SYBASE password for the Replication Server login name.

When the rs_install utility has completed running, it will have produced the following:

1 The Replication Server login SYBASE account.
2 The Replication Server's configuration file and error log.
3 The executable files to start the Replication Server.
4 Verifies that the $SYBASE/interfaces file contains the required entries.
5 Starts the Replication Server.

The installation file for the Replication Server will also contain information used to generate the Replication Server System Database, and the Replication Server System Database's Log Transfer Manager (if required).

When you use the rs_install command to generate a Replication Server, you will also be generating the Replication Server's Replication Server System Database and the Replication Server System Database's Log Transfer Manager, if required. Refer to chapter 3 for information that must be included within the installation file in order to generate the Replication Server System Database. Refer to chapter 4 for information that must be included within the installation file in order to generate a Log Transfer Manager for a Replication Server System Database.

If you are going to generate a Replication Server, its Replication Server System Database, and a Replication Server System Database Log Transfer Manager, then execute the rs_install command just once, and be sure to pass to it a single installation file that contains all the information required to generate the Replication Server, the Replication Server System Database, and the Replication Server System Database Log Transfer Manager.

3

The Replication Server System Database

The Replication Server System Database (RSSD) is a special SYBASE database within which is stored Replication Server system information, such as replication definitions, routes, and replication subscriptions. These types of Replication Server system information will be explained in later chapters. I will also explore how some types of Replication Server system information (e.g., replication definitions) are distributed throughout the Replication Server system itself.

Each and every Replication Server within the Replication system has its own Replication Server System Database. The Replication Server brings the contents of its Replication Server System Database into memory when it starts up. All changes to the contents of the Replication Server System Database have to go through the running Replication Server. In this way the Replication Server knows exactly how the contents of its Replication Server System Database have changed.

As a result of this approach to handling changes to the contents of the Replication Server System Database, the Replication Server avoids the overhead associated with having to periodically reread the contents of its Replication Server System Database during runtime.

During runtime the Replication Server also uses the Replication Server System Database to store operations information, such as information about rejected transactions and recovery information. It also uses the Replication Server System Database as an error log.

Generating a Replication Server System Database

Every time you generate a Replication Server, you must also generate its Replication Server System Database. The rs_install utility is used to generate a Replication Server System Databases. The rs_install utility takes an installation parameter file as input, as follows:

```
SYBASE/install/rs_install < installation_parameter_filename
```

The installation parameter file must contain the following information about the Replication Server System Database:

1 The sa SYBASE password for the system SQL Server.
2 The SYBASE login name of the primary user of the Replication Server System database.
3 The SYBASE password of the primary user of the Replication Server System database.
4 The SYBASE login name of the maintenance user of the Replication Server System database.
5 The SYBASE password of the maintenance user of the Replication Server System database.
6 The SYBASE login name of the database owner of the Replication Server System database.
7 The SYBASE password of the database owner of the Replication Server System database.

When the rs_install utility has completed running, it will have accomplished the following tasks in support of the Replication Server System Database:

1 It will have created the SYBASE account of the primary user of the Replication Server System database.
2 It will have created the SYBASE account of the maintenance user of the Replication Server System database.
3 It will have created the Replication Server System Database.
4 It will have loaded the system tables into the Replication Server System Database.

A given Replication Server System Database may or may not require its own Log Transfer Manager. If it does require its own Log Transfer Manager, then the installation file must contain the information the rs_install utility needs to generate the Replication Server System Database's Log Transfer Manger. Refer to chapter 4 for information that must be included within the installation file in order to generate a Log Transfer Manager for a Replication Server System Database.

The Replication Server System Database tables

The Replication Server System Database contains the following tables:

rs_classes	This table holds the names of function classes and error classes.
rs_columns	This table holds information about the columns of replication definitions.
rs_config	This table holds a set of configuration parameter values.
rs_databases	This table holds the names of databases known at a Replication Server site.
rs_debugconfig	This table same as rs_config, but is used when the Replication Server is run in debug mode.
rs_diskpartitions	This table holds information about the disk partitions used by the stable queues.
rs_erroractions	This table maps a SQL Server error number to an action to be taken by the Replication Server.
rs_exceptscmd	This table holds information used to retrieve the text of transactions from the exceptions log.
rs_exceptshdr	This table holds information about failed transactions.
rs_exceptlast	This table holds information about the last logged transaction written into the exceptions log.
rs_functions	This table holds information about Replication Server functions.
rs_funcstrings	This table holds information about Replication Server functions strings.
rs_idnames	This table holds the names of Replication Servers and SQL Server databases known to the ID Server.
rs_ids	This table holds the last identifier used for various types of Replication Server objects.
rs_locator	This table holds the last locater field received by stable queues from each of their senders.
rs_maintusers	This table holds the user login names and passwords the Replication Server uses to access other Replication Servers and SQL Servers.
rs_objects	This table holds one row for each replication definition.
rs_oqid	This table holds the last queue ID received from an origin site.

rs_queuemsg	This table holds the contents of dumped stable queues.
rs_queues	This table holds information used by the Replication Server stable queue manager and guaranteed delivery system to allow site recovery.
rs_queuemsgtext	This table holds the command or text portion of messages in dumped stable queues.
rs_recovery	This table holds actions that must be performed by the Replication Server upon recovery.
rs_repdbs	This table holds information about all SQL Server databases known by a primary Replication Server.
rs_repobjs	This table holds autocorrection flag for replication definitions at each replicate Replication Server.
rs_routes	This table holds routing information.
rs_rules	This table holds subscription rules.
rs_segments	This table holds information about the allocation of each segment.
rs_sites	This table holds information about the names of the Replication Servers known at a site.
rs_subscriptions	This table holds information about subscriptions, triggers and fragments.
rs_systext	This table holds the text of repeating groups for other Replication Server System Database tables.
rs_users	This table holds information about users with access to the Replication Server.

All tables within the Replication Server System Database are maintained using Replication Construct Language commands. Except for the rs_config table, be sure that you do not directly update tables within the Replication Server System Database. Directly updating the tables within the Replication Server System Database might well force you to reinstall the Replication Server product, and might even force you to rebuild the entire Replication Server system.

SYBASE Logins that can update the Replication Server System Database

Replication Servers use the RSSD_prim_user login name and password for Replication Server System Database updates that are replicated to other sites, such as those related to replication definitions.

Replication Servers use the RSSD_maint_user login name and password for RSSD updates that are not replicated to other sites, such as those related to rejected transactions.

Placement of the Replication Server System Database

There are no hard and fast rules for the placing of the Replication Server System Database. Any SQL Server that is near the Replication Server should be suitable. The only minimum requirement is that the SQL Server you choose must be at least a 4.9.2 SQL Server against which the necessary emergency bug fixes (EBFs) have been applied. These emergency bug fixes are required in order to upgrade the SQL Server so that it is capable of supporting the Replication Server System Database.

To determine the location of a given Replication Server's Replication Server System Database, log on to the Replication Server and enter the command admin rssd_name. This command will tell you the name and location of the Replication Server System Database.

Replication Server System Database requirements of the SQL Server

Each Replication Server System Database consumes system resources. Therefore, each Replication Server System Database has these minimum system resource requirements:

1. The SQL Server that supports the Replication Server System Database must have at least 10MB of free disk space available for the Replication Server System Database, and another 10MB available for the Replication Server System Database's transaction log.
2. The Replication Server System Database needs twenty dedicated user connections to the SQL Server that manages it.
3. There must be at least one Replication Server System Database user connection to the SQL Server for every Replication Server Monitor in the system.

Replication Server System Database for a replicant Replication Server

In addition to serving its general information requirements, a replicant Replication Server accesses its own Replication Server System Database to obtain the following information:

- Replication definition information for remote sites
- Local subscription information
- Global routing information
- Local function call and function string information
- Local error class information

In this way the Replication Server System Database supports the local customization of Replication Server behavior.

4

Log Transfer Manager

The Log Transfer Manager is an Open Server/Open Client application that monitors a SQL Server's transaction log, detects changes to a primary SQL Server database, and passes those changes onto a Replication Server process. Within UNIX environments, the Log Transfer Manager executes as a heavyweight process.

Log Transfer Manager internals

The Log Transfer Manager processes the primary database's transaction log, and transfers transactions, and asynchronous transaction executions, to the primary database's Replication Server for subsequent distribution to target databases.

A Log Transfer Manager processes a transaction log and transfers its contents to a Replication Server in the following manner:

1. The Log Transfer Manager establishes an Open Client connection to its primary SQL Server. Normally, to establish this connection the Log Transfer Manager uses the database owner login name DB_DBO_user and its password. However, if DB_DBO_user is not included within the primary database's parameters file, the Log Transfer Manager can use the SQL Server sa login name and password to establish this connection.
2. To set the Log Transfer Manager *secondary truncation point* within the primary database's transaction log (that is, the syslogs heap table), the Log Transfer Manager executes the dbcc settrunc command on the SQL Server. An important function of the Log Transfer Manager's secondary truncation point is to keep the SQL Server from truncating records that have not yet been scanned, and examined, for replication.

3. By executing the dbcc log transfer command, the Log Transfer Manager requests a scan of the primary database's transaction log. Unfortunately, the frequency at which the Log Transfer Manager requests a scan of the primary database's transaction log is not a tuneable parameter.
4. The Log Transfer Manager searches the transaction log scan and picks out the transactions that are for tables or replicated stored procedures (RPCs) that have been marked for replication.
5. The Log Transfer Manager filters out operations executed under the DB_Maint_user login name. The Replication Server uses the DB_Maint_user login name (and password) when modifying replicated data. This login name must be given all permissions needed on replicated data and on all replicated remote stored procedures. If needed, rs_setup_db creates this user login account, but it does not grant the needed permissions to replicated tables or stored procedures. The Log Transfer Manager does this filtering so that transactions executed by this login name against replicated data are not infinitely redistributed to the Replication Server. The functionality of this filtering tool is normally retained within an Replication Server system. However, this filtering mechanism can be disabled by starting the Log Transfer Manager with the -A flag.
6. For each transaction that passed through the filter, the Log Transfer Manager creates a globally unique transaction ID, and a "unique-within-the-log" origin queue ID for each log record that makes up the transaction.
7. These log records are bundled these into Log Transfer Language (LTL) commands.
8. Via the Log Transfer Manager USER thread (another Open Client connection established by the Log Transfer Manager), the Log Transfer Manager uses the LTM_RS_user login name and password and passes the LTL to the local Replication Server. The Replication Server uses subscriptions to determine where to distribute the transaction. If there are no subscriptions for a given table transaction or Remote Procedure Call, then the table transaction or Remote Procedure Call is discarded by the Replication Server.

In this way the Log Transfer Manager advances through the transaction log, starting at the location at which the secondary truncation point was initially set. Overtime, as log records are scanned from the transaction log and passed on to the local Replication Server, the Log

Transfer Manager advances the secondary truncation point to reflect the fact that certain transactions have already been passed to the Replication Server. Unfortunately, the rate at which the Log Transfer Manager advances the log truncation point is not a tunable parameter. As the secondary truncation point is advanced, the SQL Server can advance its primary truncation point, and truncate the transaction log of log records that have been scanned and examined by the Log Transfer Manager.

Generating a Log Transfer Manager for an SQL Server Database

In order to assimilate an SQL Server database into the Replication system, you must use the rs_setup_db utility. The rs_setup_db utility takes a database parameter file as input. It is within the database parameter file that you provide required information on the SQL Server database and on its Log Transfer Manager (if required). Any SQL Server database that is the source of data or stored procedures (within a Replication system) requires a Log Transfer Manager dedicated to itself.

The rs_setup_db utility takes a database parameter file as input, as follows:

```
$SYBASE/install/rs_setup_db < database_parameter_filename
```

A Log Transfer Manager's database parameter file must contain:

1. The name of the SQL Server database Log Transfer Manager.
2. The Replication Server login name the Replication Server System database Log Transfer Manager will use when it connects to the Replication Server. The default login name is LTM_RS_user.
3. The password for the LTM_RS_user login name.
4. The Replication Server System database Log Transfer Manager administrator login name. The default is LTM_admin_user.
5. The password of the LTM_admin_user login name.
6. The name of the host computer on which the Log Transfer Manager process will run.
7. The master port number for the SQL Server database Log Transfer Manager.
8. The query port number of the SQL Server database Log Transfer Manager (which is the same number as the master port).

When the rs_setup_db utility has completed running, it will have produced the following:

1. The Log Transfer Manager's configuration file and error log.
2. The LTM_RS_user account.
3. The executable file (the shell script) to start the Log Transfer Manager.
4. Verification that the $SYBASE/interfaces file contains the required entries.
5. The rs_setup_db utility then starts the Log Transfer Manager.

The LTM_admin_user login name is used when starting or shutting down an SQL Server database Log Transfer Manager.

The SQL Server database Log Transfer Manager uses the database owner's login name and password to read the SQL Server database's transaction log. If this login name is not included within the database setup file, then the Log Transfer Manager uses the sa login name and password to scan the SQL Server database's transaction log.

Generating a Log Transfer Manager for a Replication Server System Database

If the Replication Server:

- Has primary data
- Submits asynchronous transactions
- Serves as an intermediate site in an indirect route

then that Replication Server's Replication Server System Database requires a Log Transfer Manager. The purpose of the RSSD's Log Transfer Manager is to scan, examine, and submit log records of changes to replication system tables from the Replication Server System Database's transaction log, and then pass them on to the Replication Server.

The rs_install utility is also used to generate a Log Transfer Manager for a Replication Server System Database. The rs_install utility takes an installation parameter file as input, as follows:

```
$SYBASE/install/rs_install < installation_parameter_filename
```

The rs_install utility's installation parameter file for a Replication Server System Database's Log Transfer Manager must contain:

1. The name of the Replication Server System database Log Transfer Manager.
2. The Replication Server login name the Replication Server System database Log Transfer Manager will use when it connects to the Replication Server. The default login name is LTM_RS_user.
3. The password for the LTM_RS_user login name.
4. The Replication Server System database Log Transfer Manager administrator login name. The default is LTM_admin_user.
5. The password of the LTM_admin_user login name.
6. The name of the Replication Server System Database Log Transfer Manager.
7. The name of the host computer on which the Log Transfer Manager process will run.
8. The master port number for the Replication Server System Database Log Transfer Manager.
9. The query port number of the Replication Server System Database Log Transfer Manager (which is the same number as the master port).

When the rs_install utility has completed running, it will have produced the following:

1. The Replication Server System Database Log Transfer Manager's configuration file, and error log.
2. The executable files to start the Replication Server System database Log Transfer Manager.
3. Verification that the $SYBASE/interfaces file contains the required entries.
4. The rs_install utility then starts the Replication Server System database Log Transfer Manager.

The LTM_admin_user login name is used when starting or shutting down the Replication Server System database Log Transfer Manager.

The Replication Server System database Log Transfer Manager uses the LTM_RS_user login name and password to establish an Open Client connection to the Replication Server.

The Replication Server System database Log Transfer Manager uses the RSSD_DBO_user login name and password to read the Replication Server System database's transaction log. If this login name is not included within the Replication Server System database configuration file, then the Log Transfer Manager uses the sa login name and RSSD_sa_passwd to scan the Replication Server System database's transaction log.

Log Transfer Language

Log Transfer Language (LTL) is a subset of the Replication Command Language (RCL). Log Transfer Language conveys information the Replication Server needs in order to ensure that:

1. SQL Server transaction log records are reliably transferred without loss or duplication in event of failure(s).
2. Target SQL Servers execute the replicated transaction as a single logical unit of work.

When the Log Transfer Manager conveys information to a Replication Server, the physical form of the Log Transaction Language construct is dependent on the type of log record that has been scanned.

If the database transaction is a delete statement, then the before image of the affected row is submitted to the Replication Server. If the database transaction is an insert statement, then the after image of the affected row is submitted to the Replication Server. If the database transaction is an update statement, then the both the before and after images of the affected row are provided to the Replication Server. It is within the before and after images of the affected row that the data intended for distribution is contained.

When the Log Transfer Manager conveys information about replicated stored procedures (RPCs) to the Replication Server, only the identity of the replicated stored procedure and its parameters are passed to the Replication Server (the before and after images of the affected row are not passed). This significant reduction in the number of Log Transfer Language strings has the positive effect of significantly reducing network traffic within the replication domain.

The use of replicated stored procedure-type transactions can reduce overall processing time when the majority of transactions are updates to the primary database. Unlike Structured Query Language (SQL) statements, stored procedures are preparsed before they are executed. The fact that they are already parsed reduces their overall processing time relative to an equivalent Structured Query Language statement.

Estimating Log Transfer Manager memory requirements

Log Transfer Managers consume RAM. Just how much they consume depends upon the size of the largest open transaction.

A Log Transfer Manager keeps in memory the context of every transaction since the oldest open transaction. Bear in mind that the oldest open transaction does not have to be a transaction that updates a replicated table, or that contains a replicated remote procedure call. The Log Transfer Manager scans all log records, and has to examine each and every scanned log record in order to determine if a replicated table or replicated remote procedure call is associated with a given log record.

Log Transfer Manager memory requirements are broken into two components:

- The largest amount of data the Log Transfer Manager maintains in RAM
- The base minimum requirements for fixed data structures (4MB)

A useful formula for approximating Log Transfer Manager memory usage is:

```
(TR * DOLT * LTMTO).
```

Where:

TR = TransactionRate = the number of transactions per time period for the system.

DOLT = DurationOfLongestTransaction = based on the system's actual performance.

LTMTO = LogTransferManagerTransactionOverhead = 250 bytes.

To start with, you should assume that at each Log Transfer Manager will consume at least 5MB of RAM.

Log Transfer Managers also consume RAM in order to support their Open Client connection to the Replication Server. Every Log Transfer Manager connection to an Replication Server will consume, at minimum, 500K of memory. This quantity of consumed RAM will increase as the configured value of the Replication Server's Stable Queue Transaction Interface cache (sqt_max_cache_size) is increased.

The Log Transfer Manager's -A flag

The Log Transfer Manager can be started using the -A flag as a parameter to the start command. You use the LTM_admin_user login name and password when starting, and shutting down, a Log Transfer Manager. Passing the -A flag to the ltm utility (i.e., you use the ltm utility to start a Log Transfer Manager) forces the Log Transfer Manager to submit all transactions to the Replication Server just as if they were made by a client application. As a consequence, all transactions against replicated data made by the DB_Maint_user login are redistributed in the same manner as a transaction against primary data made by any authorized login. Recall that, by default, the Log Transfer Manager filters out all transaction made by the DB_Maint_user login. Therefore, do not start the Log Transfer Manager with the -A flag if:

- The primary database site is, by default, allowed to resubscribe to their primary data. If the primary site does, and if you start the Log Transfer Manager with the -A flag, then primary database transactions will infinitely loop through the local Replication Server system, e.g., primary SQL Server, to Log Transfer Manager, to Replication Server, to primary SQL Server, to Log Transfer Manager, etc.
- You intend to permit applications to update consolidated replicate tables where the consolidated replicate table is described by a replication definition and other sites can subscribe to the consolidated table. Because the Log Transfer Manager will process the consolidated replicate table as if it were primary data, be sure that all updates to the consolidated replicate table originate from their primary site(s).

5

The ID Server

The ID Server is a special Replication Server (RS) within a Replication Server domain. The function of the ID Server is to register all Replication Servers and all SQL Server databases within the Replication system.

Within a Replication system, the ID Server must be the first Replication Server to be installed, and it must be the first Replication Server that is running whenever the Replication system is brought on line.

Generating the ID Server

To establish an ID Server, you must choose a specific Replication Server to be the ID Server. There are no hard and fast rules for deciding which Replication Server to choose, but you must select one. The Replication Server you choose is usually the first Replication Server you generate, as the ID Server must be running before any other Replication Servers are started within the Replication system.

The rs_install utility is used to generate the ID Server. The rs_install utility takes an installation parameter file as input, as follows:

```
$SYBASE/install/rs_install < installation_parameter_filename
```

Before you start to generate the ID Server, make certain that:

1 You have loaded the SYBASE Replication Server software from the distribution media provided to you by the vendor.

2 All SQL Servers used to store primary data are at version 4.92 or later, and are at the Emergency Bug Fix (EBF) level indicated in your SYBASE Replication Server Release Bulletin.

3 The SYBASE environment variable (on the host computer on which you have loaded the SYBASE Replication Server software) is set to the correct SYBASE directory.

The ID Server's installation parameter file must contain:

1 The globally unique name of the ID Server. Each Replication Server name must be unique within the Replication system.

2 A Boolean variable that indicates whether the ID Server will manage SQL Server databases with primary data, may submit asynchronous transactions, and/or may serve as an intermediate site in an indirect route. Alternatively, the ID Server will merely manage SQL Server databases with primary data.

3. The full path name of the first raw disk partition (that is at least 20MB in size) for the ID Server's stable queue(s). Additional raw disk partitions can be added to the Replication Server after the Replication Server is installed.
4. A logical identifier name for the first raw disk partition.
5. The size, in megabytes, of the first raw disk partition.
6. The ID Server login name that other Replication Servers will use to connect to the ID Server.
7. The SYBASE password for the ID Server login name.

When the rs_install utility has completed running, it will have produced the following:

1. The ID Server login SYBASE account.
2. The ID Server's configuration file and error log.
3. The executable files to start the ID Server.
4. Verification that the $SYBASE/interfaces file contains the required entries.
5. The utility then starts the ID Server.

The installation file for the ID Server will also contain information used to generate the Replication Server System Database, and the Replication Server System Database's Log Transfer Manager (if required).

When you use the rs_install command to generate a Replication Server, you will also be generating the Replication Server's Replication Server System Database and the Replication Server System Database's Log Transfer Manager, if required. Refer to chapter 3 for information that must be included within the installation file in order to generate the Replication Server System Database. Refer to chapter 4 for information that must be included within the installation file in order to generate a Log Transfer Manager for a Replication Server System Database.

If you are going to generate a Replication Server, its Replication Server System Database, and a Replication Server System Database Log Transfer Manager, then execute the rs_install command just once, and be sure to pass to it a single installation file that contains all the information required to generate the Replication Server, the Replication Server System Database, and the Replication Server System Database Log Transfer Manager.

At present, there is no command you can execute that will tell you which Replication Server is the ID Server. There is, however, a way to get beyond this "product feature." Whenever you create an interfaces file, ID Server information must be added to every interfaces file; if you place a comment alongside the entry for the Replication Server that is the ID Server, you can (by reading any interfaces file) determine which Replication Server is the ID Server.

ID Server domain

A given replication system is limited to a given domain. Each replication system domain has one and only one ID Server. The SYBASE Replication Server product does not support:

1. The exchange of transactions and/or data between ID Server domains.
2. A Replication Server being managed by two or more ID Servers.
3. Multiple connections to the same SQL Server database from different ID Server domains.

However, it is possible to support multiple ID Server domains. This option is justifiable when there are no business requirements for sharing data between domains.

Operational constraints

The ID Server must be running whenever the following conditions exist:

1. An SQL Server database connection is created.
2. An SQL Server database connection is dropped.
3. A replication system route is created.
4. A replication system route is dropped.
5. An SQL Server database is added to the replication system. A given database is within one, and only one, ID Server domain. Therefore, you cannot create connections to a given database from different ID Server domains.
6. An SQL Server database is removed from the replication system.
7. A Replication Server is added to the replication system.
8. A Replication Server is dropped from the replication system.

Under normal startup conditions, and during recovery situations, SQL Servers attempt to connect with the ID Server in order to register themselves and their databases (that are active participants in the replication system). Therefore, if the ID Server is not available, it is not possible for SQL Servers to register themselves and their databases with the Replication System. SQL Servers connect to the ID Server via the ID_Server_user login name and password.

Under normal startup conditions, and during recovery situations, Replication Servers attempt to connect with the ID Server in order to register themselves. Therefore, if the ID Server is not available, it is not possible for Replication Servers to register themselves with the Replication System. Replication Servers connect to the ID Server via the ID_Server_user login name and password.

6

Stable Queues

A Stable Queue (SQ) is used by the Replication Server (RS) to spool messages:

- to another Replication Server
- to an SQL Server database
- from a Log Transfer Manager
- related to subscription materialization and dematerialization

Messages reside among these suites of stable queues until they are delivered to a remote Replication Server by a Replication Server Interface thread, or until they are delivered to an SQL Server by a Data Server Interface thread.

Stable queues are located on partitions. A partition is a physical device name used by the Replication Server. The system tables rs_diskpartitions and rs_segments contain information about raw disk partitions. A "logical partition" is merely the name assigned to a disk partition, which is, of course, a subdivision of a disk drive that can be treated for programming purposes as a separate disk drive.

A stable queue is composed of one or more 1MB segments. A segment can be allocated to one, and only one, stable queue. Therefore, different stable queues cannot share the same segment. Each segment contains sixty-four 16K blocks. A block is a unit of transfer between buffer cache and disk. A given block may contain one or more messages.

Space can be added to (and deleted from) stable queues dynamically during runtime by allocating or reallocating segments. However, a segment cannot be reallocated until all blocks that have been transferred to it are deleted.

Log Transfer Manager stable queue usage

During runtime you can determine how much space each inbound Log Transfer Manager stable queue is consuming. You can make this determination as the Replication Server System Database sa login account by executing the following query:

```
use RSSD
go

select dsname, dbname, sum(used_flag) #segs
from rs_segments, rs_databases
where rs_databases.dbid = rs_segments.q_number
and rs_segments.q_type = 1
group by dsname, dbname
go
```

A stable queue can fill up when a destination site is down, e.g., when a route or a connection is suspended. When a downstream stable queue fills up, the upstream stable queue(s) begin(s) to fill up. This upstream backflow process ripples back towards all relevant Executor thread stable queues. In the worst case, the corresponding Log Transfer Manager secondary truncation points will stagnate. That is, the Log Transfer Manager will detect that there is no free space on the Executor's inbound stable queue to hold further messages. Once the Log Transfer Manager realizes that there is no space on the Executor's stable queue, the Log Transfer Manager will stop scanning the SQL Server's source database's transaction log. When the Log Transfer Manager stops scanning, the process that causes the secondary truncation point to advance stops. A secondary truncation point that is not advancing is stagnating.

When a Log Transfer Manager's secondary truncation point stagnates, the corresponding source SQL Server will not advance the source database transaction log's primary truncation point; that is, the primary truncation point will also stagnate.

Normally, the SQL Server administration commands are used to delete old log records from the source database's transaction log. As old log records are deleted from the transaction log, the SQL Server reclaims transaction log space for new and future log records.

The SQL Server uses the location of the database transaction log's primary truncation point (and other log record status information) to determine which transaction log space to reclaim. If the log records are no longer needed by the SQL Server to assist in recovering the source database to a point of consistency (after a potential media, system, or transaction failure event), the SQL Server will remove the inactive log records from the transaction log, and advance the primary truncation point past the last purged log records.

Once a database has been brought under the control of the Replication System, the SQL Server that manages the database will not delete log records if they have not been scanned and examined by the corresponding database's Log Transfer Manager. The SQL Server identifies which log records have been scanned and examined (by the Log Transfer Manager) by determining the location of the secondary truncation point within the source database's transaction log. To ensure that the Log Transfer Manager has the opportunity to scan and examine each and every log record, the SQL Server will not advance the primary truncation point past the location of the secondary truncation point. If the SQL Server did advance the primary truncation point past the location of the secondary truncation point, then log records would be deleted before the Log Transfer Manager has scanned and examined them.

When the SQL Server is not able to advance the primary truncation point, the source database's transaction log will fill up. Once a source SQL Server database's transaction log fills up, modification transactions submitted to the SQL Server will fail. They will fail because when there is no free space in a transaction log to record the transaction, the source SQL Server will reject the transaction.

The SQL Server will only accept an authorized modification transaction if there is space in the database's transaction on which to record the database operation. Any transaction that modifies the database must be logged so that the database can be recovered to a point of consistency after a failure event. In order to protect the integrity of the database, the SQL Server will reject all modification transactions once the database's transaction log runs out of available space.

Once a transaction log runs out of available space, the database administrator may be forced, in order to allow database operations to proceed, to override the secondary truncation point and truncate the source database's transaction log. If this secondary truncation point override event occurs, you have, in all likelihood, lost transactions that have not been scanned or examined by the database's corresponding Log Transfer Manager. The first sane thing to acknowledge is that you may have lost transactions. Play it safe and assume that you have in fact lost transactions, until you can prove that the Replication system has not lost any transactions.

Most often, the net effect of a secondary truncation point override event is that the Replication system has lost transactions. Whenever transactions are lost within the Replication system, the consistency of all replicate databases, downstream from the site at which the secondary truncation point override event occurred, is gone. The second sane thing to do is to acknowledge the probability that the downstream databases may have lost consistency. Losing database consistency is a serious problem. The heuristics you will need to follow to recover the consistency of the effected downstream databases is specific to the design of your Replication system.

Stable Queue capacity planning

One critically important replication system design task, a task that minimizes the possibility of the occurrence of a secondary truncation point override event, is stable queue capacity planning. Do not estimate stable queue capacity in a negligent manner. That is, do not cut corners during the capacity planning exercise. Be absolutely sure to analyze every transaction that will update, insert, or delete data in all tables have been marked for replication. Unless you are rigorous in your capacity planning efforts, you are basing the integrity of the entire Replication system on false assumptions. Remember, it only takes one secondary truncation point override event to trash your Replication system. So much for the reading of the riot act. There is no escaping the "garbage in, garbage out" rule.

To determine the amount of disk space you need to allocate to your system, you must know the total number of replication sites within the Replication system. In addition, at each site that holds source data, you need to know the following things:

1. The length of time you want to retain messages in the stable queue(s) in the event that a downstream stable queue is unavailable.
2. The Data Manipulation Language (DML) statements that will modify data in the source database that has been marked for replication, the frequency (per second) of these transactions, and their average processing duration in seconds. As one or more transactions can make up a single logical unit of work, it is also important to know the relationship of the begin and commit commands to your suite of DML statements.
3. The identity of the tables within the source database that have been marked for replication. For each of these tables, you will have to know their row widths (in bytes), and the length of the column name(s).
4. The predicate expression (that is, the "where" clause) of each subscription to each replicated source table. This will tell you

the size of the horizontal and vertical fragments (in bytes) from the source tables that will be stored on the stable queues.

5 The volume of data in each source table, and the relationship between this data volume and the predicate expressions of each subscription to each replicated source table. This will tell you the size of the materialization stable queue that will be established to initialize the replicate tables with their copies of the source data.

6 For every site within the Replication system, you must know the identity of the local stored procedures that have been marked for replication. Specifically, you will need to know the:

- **6.1** Widths of their parameters (in bytes).
- **6.2** Length of each parameter's name.
- **6.3** Frequency (per second) of each replicated stored procedure.
- **6.4** Average processing duration in seconds of each replicated stored procedure.

Once you have all of these facts in hand, the first thing to do is to calculate the sizes of the inbound and outbound messages, for each participating site, produced by all logical units of work that modify source data marked for replication.

Calculating the sizes of the inbound and the outbound messages

To calculate the sizes of the inbound and outbound messages, start by breaking down each logical unit of work into atomic update, insert, and delete statements. For each insert and delete statement, determine the size of the inbound and outbound messages accordingly:

InboundMessageSizeInsert =
MessageOverhead + *TableRowWidth* + *LengthOfColumnNames*

InboundMessageSizeDelete =
MessageOverhead + *TableRowWidth* + *LengthOfColumnNames*

OutboundMessageSizeInsert =
MessageOverhead + *TableRowWidth* + (*NumberOfTargetSites* * 5)

OutboundMessageSizeDelete =
MessageOverhead + *TableRowWidth* + (*NumberOfTargetSites* * 5)

Update commands are treated differently from insert or delete statements because both the before and after images of the modified table row are recorded within the SQL Server transaction log. As the Log

Transfer Manager scans the SQL Server transaction log, it will pass both log records onto the Replication Server. For each update statement, determine the size of the inbound and outbound messages accordingly:

InboundMessageSizeUpdate =
MessageOverhead + (*TableRowWidth* * 2) +(*LengthOfColumnNames* * 2)
OutboundMessageSizeUpdate =
MessageOverhead + (*TableRowWidth* * 2) + (*NumberOfTargetSites* * 5)

To determine the message size of stored procedures marked for replication, sometimes referred to as functions, use the following calculation:

InboundMessageSizeFunction =
MessageOverhead + WidthOfParameters + (TableRowWidth * 2) +
LengthOfColumnNames + LengthOfParameterNames
OutboundMessageSizeFunction =
MessageOverhead + WidthOfParameters + (NumberOfTargetSites * 5)

For replicated stored procedures that update table rows, both the before and after log record are kept on the Replication Server's inbound queue, but not on the outbound queue. For the logical unit of work's begin and commit commands, use the following rules:

InboundMessageSizeBegin = *OutboundMessageSizeBegin* = 250 bytes
InboundMessageSizeCommit = *OutboundMessageSizeCommit* = 200 bytes

Each statement that a Log Transfer Manager submits to a Replication Server contains information the Replication Server needs in order to ensure that the SQL Server transaction log records are reliably transferred without loss or duplication in the event of a failure, and to ensure that the target SQL Servers will execute the replicated transaction as a single logical unit of work. The overhead of this additional information is handled via the MessageOverhead parameter. Set the value of the MessageOverhead parameter to be 200 bytes in size.

Next, you need to determine the frequency at which these individual commands and replicated stored procedures execute against a given table that has been marked for replication. We will name the frequency at which each command and procedure executes as *ChangeRate*. You will have, per table, a separate *ChangeRate* for each command and procedure that modifies that table. Depending upon the variety of logical units of work, you may well have more than one *ChangeRate* for a given command or procedure. For example, you could have two separate logical units of work, each with a different *ChangeRate*, that both insert a row into the table. If that is the case, you will need to note both cases of the insert command, each with their own separate *ChangeRate*. When assigning values to *Change Rate* parameters, be sure to assign a value to each *ChangeRate* that is greater than the maximum frequency you have observed.

Estimating source data volumes

Once you know the *ChangeRates* and the size of the inbound and outbound messages, you will be able to estimate the volume of data (in bytes) that each table that has been marked for replication will replicate. To estimate the total volume of messages generated in a database, for a given table, use the following summing approaches:

InboundTableVolume =
((*InboundMessageSizeFunction* * *ChangeRateFunction*) +
(*InboundMessageSizeInsert* * *ChangeRateInsert*) +
(*InboundMessageSizeDelete* * *ChangeRateDelete*) +
(*InboundMessageSizeUpdate* * *ChangeRateUpdate*) +etc., etc.)

OutboundTableVolume =
((*OutboundMessageSizeFunction* * *ChangeRateFunction*) +
(*OutboundMessageSizeInsert* * *ChangeRateInsert*) +
(*OutboundMessageSizeDelete* * *ChangeRateDelete*) +
(*OutboundMessageSizeUpdate* * *ChangeRateUpdate*) +
etc., etc.)

Calculating transaction volumes

Next, you will need to estimate the total number of inbound and outbound logical units of work. You need to know the frequency, or rate, at which individual logical units of work are submitted to the database's SQL Server per a given period of time. When determining *InboundTransactionRate*, be sure to include those logical units of work that do not modify replicated tables, as well as those that do modify replicated tables. After they are on the inbound queue, the Replication Server will separate the relevant log records from the nonrelevant log records. Also, base *InboundTransactionRate* on the same duration of time you used to determine *ChangeRate* for individual tables. To determine the volume of inbound logical units of work, use the following equation:

InboundTransactionVolume =
(*InboundMessageSizeBegin* + *InboundMessageSizeCommit*) *
InboundTransactionRate

To determine the volume of outbound logical units of work for each individual outbound stable queue, use the following equation:

OutboundTransactionVolume =
(*OutboundMessageSizeBegin* + *OutboundMessageSizeCommit*) *
OutboundTransactionRate

The value of the *OutboundTransactionRate* parameter and the value of *OutboundTransactionVolume* are specific to each outbound queue.

The parameter *OutboundTransactionRate* is the total number of replicated logical units of work, per a given period of time, that will pass through a given outbound stable queue. Be sure to use the same period of time as the basis for figuring the *OutboundTransactionRate* that you used to base your determination of *InboundTransactionRate.*

Determining the correct value of the *OutboundTransactionRate* parameter is not an easy task. If the following facts are true:

1 The given outbound stable queue is fed by one, and only one, Log Transfer Manager.
2 All inbound transactions submitted to the SQL Server modify replicated data.
3 The given outbound stable queue is dedicated to a target site that has subscribed to all replicated data.

Then, the values of the *OutboundTransactionRate* parameter (for that particular outbound stable queue) are equal to the value you assigned to the *InboundTransactionRate* parameter of the corresponding source inbound stable queue. In addition, if all the previous facts are true, then the value of the *OutboundTransactionVolume* will be equal to the value of the *InboundTransactionVolume* parameter of the corresponding source inbound stable queue. In the real world, the values of these parameters will seldom be equal to each other. Reality tends to be a messier place.

Recall that a given Replication Server can support more than one Log Transfer Manager. However, for a particular Replication Server, only one connection is supported to a given SQL Server, and only one route is supported to any given Replication Server.

It is through connections and routes that message streams are delivered to their destination sites. One and only one Replication Server outbound stable queue supports a particular connection or a particular route.

Inherent within the design on the Replication Server is the ability to funnel message streams from multiple source SQL Server databases (or intermediate Replication Servers) to a particular connection, or to a particular route.

So, if the given outbound stable queue is fed by multiple source sites, determining the correct value of the *OutboundTransactionRate* parameter becomes a complicated task. For outbound stable queues that are fed by multiple sources, that particular outbound stable queue's *OutboundTransactionVolume* will be the sums of all *OutboundTransactionVolume* parameters for all source sites.

To determine the *OutboundTransactionVolume* of a given source site, you need to calculate the *OutboundTransactionRate* for that given source site. In order to calculate a given source site's *OutboundTransactionRate*, you need to know the following pieces of information:

1 The *InboundTransactionRate* for a given source site.
2 The percentage of the total logical units of work that modify data marked for replication at the given source site.
3 The percentage of the logical units of work that modify data marked for replication at the given source site that will end up on this particular outbound stable queue. This aspect of the problem is sometimes referred to as "replication selectivity."

For example, let's assume there is a given source site we'll call "X." For that site, the following things hold true:

1 The value of *InboundTransactionRate* is thirty-six logical units of work per time period.
2 The percentage of logical units of work to be replicated is 0.72.
3 The replication selectivity for this particular outbound stable queue is 0.43.

Then, *OutboundTransactionRate* for source site "X" for this particular outbound stable queue is equal to:

$$(36 * 0.72 * 0.43) = 11.15$$

For each source site and each outbound stable queue you must determine the correct *OutboundTransactionRate* as shown above. You should expect to observe that the values of the *OutboundTransactionRate* parameters are different for different outbound stable queues.

Using those *OutboundTransactionRate* parameters, calculate the *OutboundTransactionVolume* for each source site. Once those tasks are completed, you must determine that particular outbound stable queue volume by summing the *OutboundTransactionVolume* parameters of all source sites.

Calculating database volumes

With the outbound and inbound volumes of logical unit of work in-hand, you can move on to the next task of figuring out the value of the *InboundDatabaseVolume* parameter. The formula you should use to figure out the value of the *InboundDatabaseVolume* parameter is as follows:

```
InboundDatabaseVolume =
    sum(InboundTableVolume) + InboundTransactionVolume
```

The value of the *InboundDatabaseVolume* parameter will be used to estimate the size of a particular inbound queue.

Calculating the size of an inbound stable queue

Inherent in the architecture of the Replication Server is the ability to support multiple Log Transfer Managers. Be sure to keep these facts in mind:

1. There is one, and only one, Log Transfer Manager per source SQL Server database.
2. There is one, and only one, stable queue per Log Transfer Manager.
3. Transactions will reside on the inbound stable queue for at least as long a period of time as the amount of time it takes the largest "open" transaction to be processed by the source SQL Server. We will call this parameter that represents the largest "open" transaction *TransactionDuration* and will use seconds as our unit of measurement.
4. To promote recoverability, the Log Transfer Manager appends information to the log records that it has scanned in and examined. This appended information significantly increases the size of replicated transactions. This increase in the volume of bytes must be accounted for. We will use the constant *C* to represent that increase in transaction size. Let *C* equal 1.4.
5. Block Overhead.
6. Failure Overhead.
7. You will have to estimate the size of each inbound queue that a given Replication Server is intended to provision to the Log Transfer Managers it supports.
8. The materialization of subscription information at destination sites consumes space on inbound and outbound stable queue.

Determining the value of the largest "open" transaction is not necessarily a straightforward task. A transaction is defined to be "open" if it has not been committed, or if it has not been rolled back. Because the SQL Server is multithreaded, and because log records from multiple transactions are recorded in the SQL Server transaction log in the order in which they occurred, there is no guarantee that the inbound stable queue will not contain log records for the largest "open" transaction as well as log records for other concurrently active transactions. Therefore, you should increase the time period of the largest "open" transaction to reflect the fact that additional log records will also need to be processed during this same time period.

Another point to consider when determining the size of an inbound stable queue is the fact that messages are written onto inbound stable queues in 16K blocks. If no messages have arrived, then no blocks are initialized. If no blocks are initialized, then no blocks are written onto the inbound stable queue. However, initialized blocks are always written onto the inbound stable queue at regular intervals. If a given block is only partially filled, it will still be written at the specified period. The implication of this design fact is that, if partially filled blocks are being written, then the size of the inbound stable queue must be increased to handle the overhead of writing partially filled blocks. This problem will be referred to as block overhead.

Guessing the amount of bytes of block overhead is easy if data (marked for replication) in the source SQL Server is loaded via a continuous batch process. When a continuous process produces replication messages, several messages will arrive at the Replication Server during the same "write block" interval. These concurrent messages will, if they do not exceed 16K in total length, be written into a single block. When this is the case, there is no overhead from writing partially filled blocks, so the amount of block overhead will be zero bytes. However, as messages trickle into the SQL Server, then messages will also trickle into the Replication Server, resulting in an amount of block overhead that is greater than zero bytes. Just how much greater is a function of transaction size, transaction rate, and the "write block" interval duration.

When messages trickle in, you are faced with a nonlinear phenomenon. The main case where this type of phenomenon is a factor for consideration is when "open" transactions that are large (relative to the size of the inbound stable queue) trickle into the SQL Server. This type of phenomenon poses a very real threat to the successful management of the inbound stable queue (and potentially, to the integrity of the downstream destination sites). To realize that they pose a serious threat, you must understand the behavior of the Replication Server's Distributor thread.

The Distributor thread works with the Stable Queue Manager thread on completed transactions. The Distributor thread does not work with transactions that are open. When a completed transaction is passed over to the Distributor thread, the space it occupied on the inbound stable queue is eventually reclaimed by the Stable Queue Manager thread. Unless a transaction transitions from the state of being open to the state of being completed, it will not be automatically removed from the inbound stable queue.

Therefore, large open transactions that trickle into a Replication Server will result in large numbers of partially filled blocks hogging the stable queue real estate, and potentially consuming all available stable queue space. And, because these open transactions are never passed onward, the inbound stable queue space they occupy cannot be automatically reclaimed. If the inbound stable queue runs out of space, the Log Transfer Manager will stagnate, its secondary truncation point will not be advanced, the SQL Server database's transaction log's primary truncation point will not be advanced, and you will, as was previously explained, be "between a rock and a hard place."

It is very important that you make your own measurements to determine the block overhead at each inbound stable queue. It is not unusual for inbound stable queues to contain blocks that are only 50% full. In the real world, blocks are rarely close to being full. To determine the amount of block overhead at each stable queue, execute the admin who,sqm command on the Replication Server. This command will return the number of bytes written and the number of 16K blocks written. To determine the current block overhead, divide the number of bytes written by the number of 16K blocks written.

Another factor to consider when sizing an inbound stable queue is that downstream sites may become unavailable during runtime. In the real world, downstream sites do, in fact, become unavailable for significant periods of time. If a connection or route to a destination site fails during runtime, then all related inbound stable queues must be large enough to hold the volume of inbound transactions from their source SQL Server database that are destined for that failed site, for the time period in which the downstream site is unavailable. We will refer to this volume of bytes as "failure overhead."

The amount of bytes you assign to failure overhead is influenced by the size of the SQL Server database's transaction log and the likely space still available to the transaction log after the downstream site failure event. Remember, we always want to avoid the scenario where we have to truncate the SQL Server's transaction log of log records that have not been scanned and examined by the corresponding Log Transfer Manager.

To estimate the size of a particular inbound stable queue, you need to know the following things:

1. The inbound database volume associated with the source SQL Server database.
2. The duration, in seconds, of the largest open transaction.
3. The value, in bytes, of the block overhead (make the measurement, or give it your best guess).
4. The value, in bytes, of the failure overhead (make the measurement, or give it your best guess).

Use the following formula to calculate the size of a particular inbound stable queue:

InboundQueueSize =
(C* *InboundDatabaseVolume* * *TransactionDuration*) + *BlockOverhead* + *FailureOverhead*

Calculating the size of an outbound stable queue

Next, we can estimate the size of a particular outbound stable queue. Outbound stable queues hold messages that are destined for a SQL Server or another Replication Server. And, as we now realize, target sites can become unavailable. Keep this fact of life in mind as we continue.

As multiple SQL Server databases can be the source of messages destined for a particular outbound stable queue, estimating the size of a particular outbound stable queue is seldom a straightforward matter. Also, just as a fraction of the volume of outbound transactions from a given SQL Server database may find their way onto a particular outbound stable queue, only a fraction of the volume of data from a source SQL Server database may find its way onto a particular outbound stable queue.

For each source SQL Server database, and for each table in that database, you must determine the percentage of the volume of replicated data that will eventually be stored on a particular outbound stable queue.

With this percentage in hand, you can determine the volume of data from a specific source SQL Server database that will reside on this particular outbound stable queue. To determine that volume of data, use the following formula:

OutboundQueueVolume =
sum(*OutboundTableVolume* * *SelectivityPercentage*) +
OutboundTransactionVolume

To determine the total volume of data from all source SQL Server databases that will reside on this particular outbound stable queue, take the sum of the source specific outbound queue volumes.

Before we can estimate the size of a particular outbound queue, we need to know three more things:

1. The outbound stable queue's save interval.
2. The maximum amount of time the outbound stable queue will be expected to store messages while the destination site is unavailable. We will call this factor the failure duration.
3. The block overhead.

To determine the size of a particular outbound stable queue, use the following formula:

OutboundQueueSize =
(*TotalOutboundQueueVolume* + *BlockOverhead*) * (*FailureDuration* + *SaveInterval*)

Calculating total stable queue size

In order to determine the total amount of disk real estate your stable queues will take over per Replication Server, use the following formula:

TotalStableQueueSize = sum(*InboundQueueSize*) + sum(*OutboundQueueSize*)

It is worth pointing out that if you have multiple disk drives or disk partitions that are dedicated to support stable queues, it is not possible to specify the location of a particular stable queue to a certain disk drive or disk partition.

Creating a stable queue

The Replication Server uses raw disk partitions as stable queues. While it is possible to use operating system files as stable queues, this is not recommended. The use of operating system files is not recommended because, in the event of a system failure, stable queue messages residing within the file management system's buffer cache will be lost.

Neither the operating system, or the Replication Server, is capable of recovering the stable queue messages that were in the volatile buffer cache at the moment of the system failure event. For most UNIX operating systems, the file management subsystem's buffer cache is, by default, ten percent of RAM. While the size of the file management subsystem's buffer cache is configurable when you build the operating system kernel, this cache can amount to a significant quantity of volatile memory. The file management system will write the message stream to the buffer cache, and these messages will remain there until the buffer cache is flushed and the contents of the buffer cache are written to disk. In the event of a system failure, the entire content of the file management system buffer cache is lost and not recoverable.

The sa account should own the disk partition(s) (or operating system file(s)), and must have read and write permissions to it. No other operating system user (other than the root account), or SYBASE account, should have write permissions to the disk partition(s) (or operating system file(s)).

In order to make a disk partition available to the Replication Server for use as a stable queue, the sa account executes the command while logged on the Replication Server:

```
add partition logical_name on "physical_name" with size
size
go
```

The *logical_name* argument is the Replication Server's name for the raw disk partition. This name must conform to the following rules for a Replication Command Language identifier:

1. Identifiers can be up to thirty bytes in length.
2. The first character of the identifier must be a letter or the symbols @ or _. After the first character, identifiers can include alphabetic, numeric, or the symbols $,@,# or _.
3. No spaces may be embedded within the identifier.

The *physical_name* argument is the full operating system specification of the raw disk partition.

The size argument is the size, in megabytes, of the entire raw disk partition. Do not allocate just a portion of the raw disk partition. If you allocate just a portion of the raw disk partition, the unallocated portion will not be accessible to you. The rule is: use it or lose it.

Checking space use of stable queues

Any Replication Server user can examine how disk space is being used in support of stable queues. To receive a display of disk space utilization information, log onto a Replication Server and execute the following command:

```
admin disk_space
go
```

Materialization stable queues

Materialization stable queues are used to support subscription materialization. Each source database has its own materialization stable queue. Each destination database has its own materialization stable queue. The process(es) of subscription materialization will not be explained here (those processes are addressed in chapter 7—Replication definitions and subscriptions), but it is important to point out that stable queues play a critical role in subscription materialization. Because stable queues play such a critical support role, you must include this use of stable queues when you conduct your stable queue capacity planning exercise.

The initial movement of source data to a destination SQL Server replicate database is called subscription materialization. The initial movement of this source data is accomplished through the movement of message stream. These message streams take up temporary residence on materialization stable queues on the controlling Replication Server, as well as on the destination Replication Server (and on any Replication Server along the data route).

When estimating the space that materialization stable queues require to support the initial distribution of source data to destination databases, you must calculate the data volumes that will be produced by the materialization of each active subscriptions (at the source, as well as at the destination(s)). Be certain to extend every participating Replication Server's total queue space to include these peak data volumes.

7

Replication definitions and subscriptions

Within a replication system, there are three types of SQL Server databases:

1. A database whose only role is to serve as a source of data and/or stored procedures. I will refer to such databases as primary, or source, databases.
2. A database whose only role is to serve as a destination for replicated data and/or replicated stored procedures. I will refer to such databases as replicate, or destination, databases.
3. A database that serves as both a source of, and a destination for, replicated data and/or replicated functions. I will refer to such databases as mixed databases.

Assimilating a SQL Server database into a replication system

Before an SQL Server database can participate in a replication system, it must be prepared. Once the SQL Server database has been prepared and assimilated into a replication system, you can implement the necessary replication language constructs such as replication definitions and replication subscriptions.

Once you assimilate an SQL Server database into the replication system, you must not rename that database. If you do rename the database, you will extensively corrupt the replication system and cause the system to hang or crash at runtime.

In the process of assimilating an SQL Server database into a replication system the database must be prepared in the following ways:

1. The SQL Server that manages the database must be upgraded to work within a replication system.
2. The SQL Server database must be loaded with database objects that support the Replication Server.
3. The maintenance user SYBASE login that the controlling Replication Server will use when updating replicated data must be created. All necessary database permissions must be granted to this maintenance user.
4. A connection from the controlling Replication Server to the database's SQL Server must be created.
5. If the SQL Server database is a source of data, or of stored procedures, then a Log Transfer Manager must be built for the database.

To accomplish the first task, you will have to acquire, and apply, the necessary software upgrades. To accomplish tasks two through five, you will use the rs_setup_db utility.

The rs_setup_db utility takes a database setup file as input:

```
$SYBASE/install/rs_setup_db < db_setup_file
```

The database setup file should contain the following information:

1. The name of the Replication Server that will control this database. Note that one and only one Replication Server can control a given SQL Server database.
2. The password of the controlling Replication Server's sa login.
3. The name of the SQL Server that manages the database you are assimilating into the replication system.
4. The password of the SQL Server's sa login. The rs_setup_db utility will use the SQL Server's sa account to upload supporting class functions and supporting tables into the SQL Server database. In addition, if this particular database will be the source of data and/or stored procedures, then its corresponding Log Transfer Manager process could, as an alternative to the database owner's SYBASE login, use the SQL Server's sa account to gain access to the database's transaction log.
5. The name of the SQL Server database you are assimilating into the Replication Server.
6. Indicate whether or not the SQL Server database will need a corresponding Log Transfer Manager.
7. The SYBASE login name of the maintenance user that the controlling Replication Server will use when updating replicated data within the SQL Server database.

8. The password of the controlling Replication Server's maintenance user login.
9. The SYBASE login name of the owner of the SQL Server database. The corresponding Log Transfer Manager will, by default, use this login to gain access to the database's transaction log. If you do not include the name of the owner of the SQL Server database, then the Log Transfer Manager will use the managing SQL Server's sa login.
10. The password of the SQL Server database owner's login account if the SQL Server database requires a Log Transfer Manager.

If the SQL Server database requires a Log Transfer Manager, then this additional information must be recorded in the rs_setup_db's database setup file:

1. The SYBASE login name of a controlling Replication Server user account that Log Transfer Manager will use to log in to the controlling Replication Server.
2. The password of the controlling Replication Server user account that the Log Transfer Manager will use.
3. The SYBASE login name for the user who will start up and shut down this particular Log Transfer Manager.
4. The password of the SYBASE account that will start up and shut down this particular Log Transfer Manager.

An entry for the corresponding Log Transfer Manager needs to be placed within the interfaces file. Be certain prior to running the rs_setup_db utility that the interfaces fill contains the following information:

1. The name of the corresponding Log Transfer Manager.
2. The name of the host computer on which the Log Transfer Manager process will execute.
3. The master port number for the corresponding Log Transfer Manager.
4. The query port number for the corresponding Log Transfer Manager.

Once you have updated the interface file and have entered all of the required information into the database setup file, the rs_setup_db utility will accomplish the following things:

1. Uploading of the supporting class functions, stored procedures, and tables into the SQL Server database you are assimilating into the replication system.
2. If this particular SQL Server database needs a Log Transfer Manager, then a Log Transfer Manager configuration file and an executable shell script to start the Log Transfer Manager will be created.

3 The controlling Replication Server maintenance user SYBASE login account will be created.
4 The connection between the controlling Replication Server and the SQL Server that manages this particular database will be implemented.
5 Verification that the interfaces file contains the appropriate entries for the corresponding Log Transfer Manager.
6 Start-up of the corresponding Log Transfer Manager, if required.
7 Verification that the controlling Replication Server maintenance user can log into the SQL Server database.
8 The utility sets the Log Transfer Manager's secondary truncation point within the SQL Server database's transaction log.

The rs_setup_db utility creates and starts up the corresponding Log Transfer Manager on the machine you are logged onto when you execute the rs_setup_db utility. So, be certain to log onto the computer that will host the corresponding Log Transfer Manager before you execute the rs_setup_db utility.

The controlling Replication Server

A given SQL Server database can be controlled by one and only one Replication Server. However, a given Replication Server can control zero, one, or more than one SQL Server databases.

If the given Replication Server is controlling a source or mixed SQL Server database, then that particular Replication Server's Replication Server System Database must have a corresponding Log Transfer Manager.

Supporting database objects

When you execute the rs_setup_db utility, it creates within the SQL Server database you are assimilating the following supporting database objects:

1 The rs_lastcommit table.
2 The rs_update_lastcommit stored procedure.
3 The rs_get_lastcommit stored procedure.
4 The rs_marker system function and rs_marker stored procedure.
5 The sp_setreplicate stored procedure.

The rs_lastcommit table is used to store the last logical unit of work committed in a destination database from each source database.

The rs_update_lastcommit stored procedure is used to update the rs_lastcommit table with the identity of each logical unit of work that the Data Server Interface thread commits to the destination SQL Server database. Any SYBASE login account at a destination site that executes an asynchronous stored procedure must have permissions to execute the rs_update_lastcommit at the source database that will eventually receive the asynchronous stored procedure call.

When the Replication Server boots up, the Data Server Interface thread executes the rs_get_lastcommit stored procedure to retrieve the identity of the last logical unit of work it committed to the destination SQL Server database. The Data Server Interface thread uses the results returned by this procedure to determine the position in the message stream (stored on the destination's outbound stable queue) from which to resume submitting transactions to the destination SQL Server database.

The rs_marker system function provides the Replication Server with a means to support subscription materialization. If the particular database is a source database, then both the rs_marker system function and the rs_marker stored procedure must exist within it. All SYBASE login accounts (throughout the replication system) that have permission to create subscriptions against data in this source database must also have permission to execute the rs_marker stored procedure in the source database.

Marking a source SQL Server database table for replication

Source SQL Server databases could potentially contain tables and stored procedures that may or may not, on an individual basis, be replicated. You must mark the individual tables and stored procedures that are to be replicated. To mark a table (or stored procedure) for replication, use the following command:

```
sp_setreplicate NameOfDatabaseObject [, true | false]
```

Only the SQL Server sa account and the source database owner are authorized to execute the sp_setreplicate stored procedure.

When you execute the sp_setreplicate command with the correct parameters initialized, the systat column of the sysobjects table for the source table (or stored procedure) is updated. From that point on, whenever a transaction modifies the table (or executes the stored procedure), the SQL Server will record the updated value of the systat column on log records it writes into the transaction log. The updated value of the systat column on the log record indicates that a specific log record is marked for replication. The Log Transfer Manager will continuously forward to the controlling Replication Server all log records that are marked for replication. Unless you mark an individual table (or stored procedure) for replication, the corresponding Log Transfer Manager will not forward transactions that modify that individual table (or that execute that individual stored procedure).

The SQL Server allows you to create two or more tables with the same name in the same database, just as long as each of these tables has a different owner. For example, an SQL Server database could contain person A's table X as well as person B's table X. However, you cannot use the sp_setreplicate command to mark two or more tables with the same name for replication, even if they have different owners. Continuing with our example, you could mark person A's table X for replication, but if you then tried to mark person B's table X for replication, the second invocation of sp_setreplicate would fail.

Be certain to record the sp_setreplicate commands that mark tables and stored procedures for replication in a text file, which you can submit to the source SQL Server as required over the life of the source database.

Introduction to replication definitions

A replication definition is a formal description of a source SQL Server database table whose data you want to be replicated to one or more destination SQL Server database tables. A given source SQL Server database table can have one and only one replication definition. Also, you cannot create a replication definition against a database view.

Here's the syntax of the create replication definition command:

```
create replication definition NameOfReplicationDefinition
with primary at NameOfSQLServer.NameOfSQLServerDatabase
[with all tables named 'NameOfTable')
(NameOfColumn SYBASEDatatype [, NameOfColumn SYBASEDatatype, ...])
primary key (NameOfColumn [, NameOfColumn, ...])
[searchable columns (NameOfColumn [, NameOfColumn, ...])]
```

For the create replication definition command, the mandatory language constructs are:

1 create replication definition *NameOfReplicationDefinition*— The name you give to the replication definition must conform to the rules for identifiers, and it must be unique within the controlling Replication Server's Replication Server System Database. Identifiers can be up to thirty bytes in length. The first character of the identifier must be a letter or the symbols @ or _; after the first character identifiers can include alphabetic or numeric characters, or the symbols $,@,# or _, and no spaces may be embedded within the identifier.

2 with primary at—Specifies the source SQL Server and the source database, that manages the base table.

3 The column definition clause—The replication definition of an SQL Server database table may contain all columns within that particular table, or it may contain a subset of all columns within that particular table.

4 primary key—List of the columns that make up the base table's primary key.

For the create replication definition command, the optional language constructs are:

1 searchable columns—Limits the set of replication definition columns that can be used in all corresponding subscriptions' predicate expressions (that is, their where clauses).

2 with all tables named—Allows you to create a replication definition to tables with different names than the replication definition. If this optional construct is not used, then the name of the replication definition is automatically set to the name of the base table.

Enter create replication definition command(s) while logged onto the source SQL Server database's controlling Replication Server. Use isql (or some other custom-built Open Client-based front-end tool) to enter replication definition commands.

Whatever errors that may have occurred while executing create replication definition commands are recorded within the Replication Server error file. You should continually inspect the Replication Server error file when executing replication definition commands. Even though error messages may not appear within the Replication Server error file, you cannot assume the replication definitions are error-free. The quality of your executed replication definition commands will not be evident until you execute subscription commands against the replication definition.

When you execute the create replication definition command, the rs_delete, rs_insert, rs_select, rs_select_with_lock and rs_update default data manipulation system functions are automatically created for you.

Replication definitions are stored within the controlling Replication Server's Replication Server System Database, whose Log Transfer

Manager detects and passes on the Replication definitions to the controlling Replication Server for distribution to all Replication Server sites in the Replication Server system. The set of automatically created data manipulation system functions are distributed throughout the replication system along with their corresponding replication definition.

Be certain to record the create replication definition commands in a text file, which you can submit to the source SQL Server as required over the life of the source database.

The Replication Server Command Language and Transact-SQL

The Replication Server Command Language is in certain ways similar to the SQL Server Transact-SQL Command Language. However, there are important differences between the two command languages.

The two command languages are similar in the following ways:

1. Identifiers can be up to thirty bytes in length, and the first character of the identifier must be a letter or the symbols @ or _; after the first character, identifiers can include alphabetic or numeric characters, or the symbols $,@,# or _, and no spaces may be embedded within the identifier.
2. Comments can be delimited C-language style (that is, by /* */ pairs), or comments can be delimited ANSI-style (which consists of any character string beginning with two connected minus signs {i.e., —} and ending with a newline symbol).
3. You can break a command line string anywhere except within a keyword.
4. Extraneous white space in the command line is ignored.
5. You can continue a command line character string to the next line by using the backslash symbol (\).

The Replication Server Command Language is dissimilar to the SQL Server Transact-SQL Command Language in the following ways:

1. Replication Server Command Language identifiers may not be multibyte characters.
2. The Replication Server Command Language is not case-sensitive except for identifiers and the literal data value of character data. This is dissimilar to Transact-SQL Command Language, because case-sensitivity is determined by the SQL Server against which the Transact-SQL Command Language constructs are executing. The case-sensitivity of an SQL Server is established when that particular SQL Server is installed, or when the SQL Server sa changes the SQL Server's case-sensitivity.

3 The Replication Server Command Language does not support qualifying a table identifier with the SYBASE login name of the owner of that table. There is a good reason for this rule. The SYBASE SQL Server transaction log records do not contain the identity of the table owner. Therefore, there is no information within the transaction log that the Log Transfer Manager can examine to distinguish transactions against table X belonging to person A from transactions against table X belonging to person B.
4 Because function strings use the double quote symbol ("), you are limited, within the Replication Server Command Language, to using the single quote symbol ('). If you encounter a double quote symbol within your character string, then you must surround each double quote symbol with a pair of single quote symbols (e.g., '"').

In that you will be distributing Replication Server Command Language constructs throughout the replication system, all SQL Servers, Replication Servers, and Log Transfer Managers must use the same character set. This restriction places a serious constraint on the degree of heterogeneity among data servers within a replication system.

The replication definition name

The name of the replication definition must be the same name as its base table, and the same name of all destination tables that will hold data replicated originating from the base table. This rule does not apply if you are also using the optional with all tables named clause.

Also, the name of the replication definition must be unique throughout the replication system. However, the replication system does not enforce this rule that two replication definitions cannot have the same name. You have to police yourself on this matter. Along these lines, the create replication definition command is asynchronous; that is, it returns control to you in the form of the command line prompt immediately after you execute the command. You do not wait to regain control of the command line prompt while the function strings are made, or while the function strings and the replication definition are being distributed throughout the replication system. In that the command is asynchronous, the Replication Server does not guarantee that someone else somewhere else in the replication system is not creating a replication definition with the same name as the one you are currently creating. Keep the asynchronous aspect of the command in mind while you go about policing yourself.

The column definitions clause

Only data within the set of columns listed within the replication definition's column definition clause will be replicated. If in the column definition clause you have chosen a subset of the columns in that base table, you have created what is called a projection of the base table; sometimes it is referred to as a vertical fragment of the base table.

As you define individual base table columns, you must be aware of the following rules:

1 When specifying a base table column that is implemented as a user-defined datatype, you must specify the underlying SYBASE datatype for that column. You cannot specify the user-defined datatype of that column.

2 Not all SYBASE datatypes are fully supported by the Replication Server.

2.1 The Replication Server directly supports this subset of SYBASE datatypes: int, smallint, tinyint, float (without a specified precision), real, money, smallmoney, char(*n*), varchar(*n*), binary(*n*), varbinary(*n*), datetime, smalldatetime, and bit.

2.2 The Replication Server indirectly supports this subset of SYBASE datatypes by converting them as follows: for float (with specified precision) use real (numeric accuracy may be lost); for decimal use real (numeric accuracy may be lost); for numeric use real (numeric accuracy may be lost); for double use real (numeric accuracy may be lost); for nchar use char(n); for nvarchar use varchar(n); for timestamp use binary(8). As columns of type identity must be numeric, then use real (numeric accuracy may be lost).

2.3 Text and images are not supported by the Replication Server. Do not be misled into imagining that you can use varchar(*n*) to indirectly support these two data types. To directly or indirectly support text or image data types would require extensive modifications to the SQL Server transaction log process. First, text and image data types are enormously large (> 2GB). Because they are so huge, the SQL Server, by default, does not record them in the database's transaction log. The only means by which a Log Transfer Manager is able to scan and examine a transaction that modifies data (marked for replication) is by having that transaction recorded within the transaction log it is monitoring. In that it is possible, and actually preferred, that transactions that modify text and image data would not be recorded within a transaction log, it is possible (and actually highly probable) that such a transaction would go undetected by the responsible Log Transfer Manager. This is a serious database consistency hole that you cannot close up with certainty. Second, the SQL Server only stores within a text or image column the locally valid pointer to the location of the data pages that actually hold the text and image data. The literal data value of these pointers are only valid within the local SQL Server process, and hence are not candidates for replication; they would not point to the correct data pages at the destination SQL Server. Third, as a varchar datatype is limited to 255 bytes in length, it is not possible to ensure that all data values associated with a given text or image field will be contained within the varchar column and hence be replicated in their entirety. Even if you intend to use multiple rows of varchar columns to hold the text and image data, you still have to address the inbound stable queue problem of large "open" transactions that will likely arise from logging the large volume of text and image data through these varchar rows. Fourth, when resolving which destination sites want to receive a replicate of the text or image data, the Subscription Resolution Engine module would need access to potentially huge volumes of virtual cache just to complete its tests on text or image datatypes. Fifth, the distribution of large volumes of text and image data across a network is no small matter. To minimize network traffic, you would want to compress the text and image data prior to transmission. At present, the Replication Server does not support data compression or decompression.

3. The data types of the replication definition columns must match the datatype of the corresponding base table columns. This rule holds true unless you are providing indirect support by converting the base table column's data type.
4. The order in which you list the columns in your replication definition is important. To avoid unnecessary Executor thread processing overhead, be sure to order the columns in your

replication definition exactly as they appear in the base table. If you violate the column ordering, which you can, the Executor thread normalization process will have to reorder them so that they appear in exactly the same column order as they appear in the base table.

5 Do not define a column whose data you do not need to replicate.
6 Do not define a column that is not within the base table. Most often this rule is violated because of typos.
7 Any column that you define cannot also be listed among the searchable columns if that column is NULLABLE.

The primary key clause

As anyone who has been trained in the practice of relational database design knows, every table must have a primary key that uniquely identifies every row in the table. If you have a table that does not have a primary key associated with it, then you should place that structure outside of the relational database. However, as anyone who has implemented a physical database on an SQL Server knows, you can create tables that do not have a primary key that uniquely identifies every row in the table. If you have a table in your source database that lacks a primary key, then do not create a replication definition for it!

If you create a replication definition for a base table that lacks a primary key, then corresponding distributed transactions will fall at the destination site(s). Therefore the Replication Server, unlike the SQL Server, absolutely demands that a primary key exist for every base table for which you create a replication definition. While the Replication Server requires that a primary key exist for each and every base table, it does not check for the existence of the primary key on the base table when you create the replication definition. You have to police yourself on this matter.

To complete this suite of warnings regarding primary keys, you must not permit the literal data value of the primary key in a base table (that has been marked for replication) to be modified. Aside from the relational theory violations inherent in any modification to the literal data value of a primary key, the corresponding Log Transfer Manager will scan these updates, forward them to the controlling Replication Server, and, as a result, incorrect data will be distributed throughout the replication system.

The primary key clause is used by function strings. Without getting into too much detail right here, let's define function strings as a means for mapping the source SQL Server database command to destination data server Application Server Interface (API). Default functions strings are created automatically by the replication system. The function string contains a predicate expression (that is, a where clause), within which the replication definition's primary key clause is embedded. The Replication Server that controls the destination SQL Server database uses function string predicate expressions when applying changes to the destination replicate database.

The optional searchable columns clause

The intention of the optional searchable columns clause is to restrict the variety of subscriptions that can be written against a particular replication definition.

If you do not use the optional searchable columns clause, then all subscriptions against a particular replication definition must be for all columns contained within that particular replication definition.

If you use the optional searchable columns clause, then the predicate expression (the where clause) of all subscriptions you create against this particular replication definition can only refer to the searchable column(s).

The optional with all tables clause

Unless you use the optional with all tables clause, all destination replicate tables and the source base table(s) must have the same name as the replication definition. There are exceptions to this rule, however.

One exception allows the name of the destination table(s) to be different from the base source table. In those cases where you want to replicate data to a destination table whose name is different from the base table, you must create a view over the destination replicate table. Be certain that the view conforms to SQL Server rules governing updating views. The name of the view must be identical to the name of the base source table. All columns within the view must be within the same destination table. Also, be certain that the data types of the columns within the view's base table match (or are compatible with) the data types of the columns in the base source table. There is another exception to this rule, but I will not explore it until I have explained function strings in detail.

Pre-existence of connection and routes

Within a replication system, a connection is a message stream from a controlling Replication Server to the controlled SQL Server database, and a route is a message stream from a Replication Server to another Replication Server.

The replication system uses connections to apply distributed transactions to destination databases, and it uses routes to transport transactions and replication system information (such as replication definitions and their function strings) between Replication Servers.

Before you create a replication definition against a base table, a connection must exist between the SQL Server that manages the database that contains the base table and the controlling Replication Server. When you assimilated the source SQL Server database into the replication system, the rs_setup_db utility automatically created the necessary connection for you. To create a connection to a non-SQL Server, execute (on the controlling Replication Server, and as the controlling Replication Server sa account) the following command:

```
create connection to NameOfSQLServer.NameOfDatabase
{set error class NameOfErrorClass
set function string class NameOfFunctionStringClass
set username NameOfReplicationServerMaintenanceUser
set password PasswordOfReplicationServerMaintenanceUser}
with log transfer on
```

Replication system routes are unidirectional; that is, messages flow from point A to point B, but not both ways. The Replication Server does not support multiple direct (or indirect) routes from a given Replication Server to another given Replication Server. To create a route from one Replication Server to another Replication Server, execute (as the sa account on the "from" Replication Server, while logged on the "from" Replication Server) the following command:

```
create route to NameOfDestinationReplicationServer
{set next site to NameOfIntermediateReplicationServer |
set username NameOfReplicationServerUser
set password PasswordOfReplicationServerUser}
```

If the next site clause is omitted, then a direct route is created to the destination Replication Server. If the next site clause is used, then an indirect route to the destination Replication Server, through an intermediate Replication Server, is created. A given route can have zero, one, or many intermediate Replication Servers.

With the route in place, all replication definitions (and their function strings) you subsequently create at the controlling Replication Server are distributed to all Replication Servers within the replication system. When routes are created after replication definitions have been created, all existing replication definitions and their function strings are immediately distributed from the controlling Replication Server to all Replication Servers within the replication system once the new route is created.

The replication definition creation cycle

The creation of replication definitions is a process that passes through a linear sequence of events, as follows:

1. The `create replication definition` command is executed.
2. The controlling Replication Server creates the default functions and function strings for the replication definition.
3. The controlling Replication Server, as the Replication Server System Database user, accesses its Replication Server System Database and inserts information about the replication definition.
4. The replication definition information inserted into the Replication Server System Database is logged, and the Replication Server System Database's Log Transfer Manager scans and examines the entries.
5. The Replication Server System Database's Log Transfer Manager forwards the log records to the controlling Replication Server.
6. The default functions are distributed throughout the replication system, along with the replication definition, by the controlling Replication Server.
7. The default functions and function strings, along with the replication definition, are written into the destination site's Replication Server System Database.

This cycle must complete all of its steps before a destination site can subscribe to the source data.

Once the source table is marked to be replicated and a replication definition for that source table exists, the source database's corresponding Log Transfer Manager will forward transactions to the controlling Replication Server. If there are active subscriptions against the replication definition, then the forwarded transactions will be distributed by the controlling Replication Server. If there are no active subscriptions against the replication definition, then the controlling Replication Server will discard the forwarded transactions.

Introduction to replication subscriptions

A subscription is a formal request to receive an initial copy of source data, and to have that copy continually updated in a fully automated manner. You create subscriptions against existing replication definitions, and each replication definition can work concurrently with many subscriptions.

There are two ways for a destination replicate table to receive its initial copy of source data. The first is through one of the fully automated materialization methods. The other is through a user-supported bulk materialization approach. A create subscription command can invoke any one of the fully automated materialization methods; these are the most resource-intensive Replication Server commands.

Here's the syntax of the create subscription command that will invoke one of the fully automated materialization methods:

```
create subscription NameOfSubscription
for NameOfReplicationDefinition
with replicate at NameOfSQLServer.NameOfSQLServerDatabase
[where NameOfColumn { < ¦ > ¦ >= ¦ <= ¦ = } LiteralDataValue
[and NameOfColumn { < ¦ > ¦ >= ¦ <= ¦ = } LiteralDataValue] ...]
[without holdlock ¦ incrementally]
```

For the create subscription command, the mandatory language constructs are:

1. create subscription *NameOfSubscription*—The name you give to the subscription must conform to the rules for identifiers, and it must be unique for the destination database and the replication definition.
2. for *NameOfReplicationDefinition*—Specifies the name of the replication definition that the subscription is for.
3. with replicate at *NameOfSQLServer.NameOfSQLServerDatabase*—Specifies the destination SQL Server, and the destination database, that manages the replicate table.

For the create subscription command, the optional language constructs are:

1. where clause—Establishes the criteria by which rows in the source base table will be replicated to the subscribing site. If

this predicate expression is omitted when you create the subscription, then all rows within the source base table will be replicated to the subscribing sites. If the searchable column option was used in the source base table's replication definition, then the predicate expressions of all subscriptions you create against that particular replication definition can only refer to the searchable column(s).

2 without holdlock—Data will be selected by the destination Replication Server from the source base table without a lock being held. The without holdlock option and the incrementally option are mutually exclusive constructs.

3 incrementally—The destination Replication Server will initialize the replicate table with subscription data by submitting rows of data in batches of insert statements. The incrementally option and the without holdlock option are mutually exclusive constructs.

Here's the syntax of the define subscription command that will invoke the bulk materialization method(s):

```
define subscription NameOfSubscription
for NameOfReplicationDefinition
with replicate at NameOfSQLServer.NameOfSQLServerDatabase
[where NameOfColumn { < | > | >= | <= | = } LiteralDataValue
[and NameOfColumn { < | > | >= | <= | = } LiteralDataValue] ...]
```

With the bulk subscription materialization approach the destination Replication Server does not copy the rows of the source data to the destination database. Instead, you transfer the subscription data yourself, usually by copying the data to tape and then loading the tape at the replicate site. This is a significantly less resource-intensive approach to initializing the table that will hold the replicate data.

Enter the create subscription command(s) while logged onto the destination SQL Server database's controlling Replication Server. Use isql (or some other custom-built Open Client-based front-end tool) to enter subscription commands.

Whatever errors that may have occurred while executing subscription commands, they are recorded within the Replication Server error file. You should continually inspect the Replication Server error file when executing subscription commands. Even though error messages may not appear within the Replication Server error file, you cannot assume the subscriptions are error-free.

Subscriptions are stored within the destination's controlling Replication Server's Replication Server System Database, whose Log Transfer Manager detects and passes on the subscription to the destination's controlling Replication Server for distribution to the source SQL

Server's controlling Replication Server. A copy of the subscriptions are then stored within the source SQL Server's controlling Replication Server's Replication Server System Database.

Be certain to record the create subscription commands in a text file, which you can submit to the destination SQL Server's controlling Replication Server as required over the life of the destination database.

Cover all your bases

Before you execute the create subscription command, make sure of the following things:

1. The source base table must exist in the source database, and it must contain the columns and data types as defined in replication definition.
2. The replication definition must have been created for the source table.
3. The columns and data types used in the create subscription command must match the column names and data types in the replication definition for the table.
4. A connection from the replicate Replication Server to the replicate database must have been created.
5. The route from the Replication Server that controls the SQL Server that manages the source database to the destination Replication Server that controls the SQL Server that manages the replicate (or mixed) database must have been created. This is not required if the Replication Server that controls the source database is the same as the Replication Server that controls the replicate (or mixed) database.
6. The replication definition needs to have been replicated to the destination Replication Server's Replication Server System Database.
7. Make sure that you have the correct permissions.
8. Make sure that all connections and routes are up.
9. Make sure that a table or view with the same name and columns as the replication definition has not been created at the source database. If you have created custom function strings for the source table, make sure that they match the underlying table at the replicate. This can cause errors at the source database as a result of the destination Replication Server executing select during subscription materialization.
10. Make sure that a table or view with the same name and columns as the replication definition has not been created at the replicate database. If you have created custom function strings, make sure that they match the underlying table at the

replicate. This would cause errors returned by the replicate database when the Data Server Interface thread attempts to apply transactions held in the materialization queue.

11 If the source database does not have the rs_sqlserver_function _class, make sure that there are function strings for the rs_select function that match the predicate expression of the create subscription or define subscription command.

12 Make sure that the interface file used by the destination Replication Server has an entry for the source Replication Server, and an entry for the source SQL Server.

13 Make sure that all of the following processes and threads are up and running:

- **13.1** The SQL Server that manages the source database.
- **13.2** The Replication Server controlling the SQL Server that manages the source database.
- **13.3** The Log Transfer Manager for the source database.
- **13.4** The SQL Server that manages the replicate database.
- **13.5** The Replication Server that controls the SQL Server that manages the replicate database. This is called the destination Replication Server.
- **13.6** The connection from the replicate Replication Server to the replicate database (that is, the replicate Replication Server Data Server Interface thread to the replicate database).
- **13.7** The route between the source Replication Server and the destination Replication Server (if they are not the same server).
- **13.8** All intermediate Replication Servers in the route between the source and the destination.

14 Check the error logs for all participating data and replication servers, and make sure that there are no errors. Be sure to resolve any such errors before proceeding with subscriptions.

The subscription materialization stages

During materialization, subscriptions pass through five generic stages:

1 Definition
2 Activation
3 Build materialization queue (optional)
4 Apply materialization queue (optional)
5 Validation

However, there are a number of ways that subscriptions can pass through some, or all, of these stages:

1 Atomic materialization
2 Incremental atomic materialization
3 Nonatomic materialization
4 Any of the four methods for bulk materialization

Regardless of which of the alternative ways you elect to materialize subscriptions, the following facts apply:

1 The create subscription command returns before the data materialization is complete.
2 Be certain to use the check subscription command at both the source and destination sites to monitor the progress of the materialization.
3 Subscription materialization is only really complete when the replicate data is consistent with the source data by the time materialization completes, and the check subscription command indicates that the subscription is valid.

Atomic materialization

Atomic materialization is the default subscription materialization method for the Replication Server. With atomic materialization a holdlock is always taken on the source data table. To invoke this method do not use either the without holdlock option, or the incrementally option in your create subscription command.

If the without holdlock option is not specified, the subscription data is applied atomically and consistency is complete, except for the latency introduced by the overhead of the replication system itself. The source data rows are applied at the destination replicate table in one (potentially very large) transaction. Because the source data rows are applied as a single transaction, the replicate copy of all source data rows becomes available within the destination SQL Server database at the same point in time.

Right after you successfully execute the create subscription command, the (default subscription materialization) process of atomic materialization passes through the following phases:

1 The destination Replication Server executes the rs_select_with_lock default data manipulation system function to retrieve the source data. No data rows will materialize in the destination database until the select transaction has been completed in the source database. If the subscription specifies a large volume of source data, the select

transactions can run for a long time, causing a noticeable delay at the destination site.

2. To hold the data volumes it will receive, the destination Replication Server builds a subscription materialization stable queue.
3. Once the materialization stable queue is built, the destination Replication Server sends the activation request to the Replication Server that controls SQL Server that manages the source database.
4. The controlling Replication Server passes this activation request to the source database's SQL Server via the rs_marker system function.
5. When the source database's SQL Server receives the activation request, the subscription is marked valid within the controlling Replication Server (as well as within its Replication Server System Database).
6. All database operations against the source data, following the activation request, are forwarded to the replicate database if the modified data rows match the subscription's predicate expression.
7. The controlling Replication Server sends the activation request back to the destination Replication Server, where it is inserted into the Data Server Interface thread's outbound stable queue for the destination database's SQL Server.
8. When the Data Server Interface thread processes the activation request message, the subscription status is changed to active within the controlling Replication Server (as well as within its Replication Server System Database).
9. The Data Server Interface thread also switches over from its regular outbound stable queue for the destination database to the connection's subscription materialization stable queue. If you want to know which stable queue the Data Server Interface thread is using, then execute, on the destination Replication Server, the admin who,dsi command. The results of the admin who,dsi command will indicate which queue the Data Server Interface thread is currently processing.
10. The Data Server Interface thread then applies the messages in the connection's subscription materialization stable queue to the destination SQL Server database.
11. After the connection's subscription materialization stable queue is processed, the subscription is marked valid and the materialization is complete.

Incremental atomic materialization

The incremental atomic materialization approach is invoked by using the incrementally option of the create subscription command.

When the incrementally option is specified, the destination Replication Server applies the source data rows in batch, so that data appears at the replicate a batch at a time. The use of this batch initialization technique avoids long running open transactions; there can be a very serious problem with large source tables.

When the incrementally option is used, the select is performed (by the destination Replication Server) with a holdlock so that serial consistency with the source is maintained. The replicate table eventually passes through the states that occurred previously at the source.

As a result of using the incrementally option, queries against the replicate data may, during subscription materialization, return incomplete data sets for the subscription. This temporary condition ends when the create subscription command indicates that the subscription is valid.

The subscription materialization process for the incremental atomic materialization passes through the same phases as atomic materialization.

Nonatomic materialization

The nonatomic materialization approach is invoked by using the without holdlock option of the create subscription command. This approach differs from the atomic materialization method in that the nonatomic materialization approach uses the rs_select default data manipulation system function rather than rs_select_with_lock default data manipulation system function to retrieve data from the source database.

When the without holdlock option is specified, the destination Replication Server applies the source data rows in batch, so that data appears at the replicate a batch at a time. The use of this batch initialization technique avoids long running open transactions; there can be a very serious problem with large source tables.

The without holdlock option has a direct effect on how data will be initialized within the destination replicate table. If the without holdlock option is specified, materialization rows are selected from the source without a holdlock, which can introduce inconsistency because the rows may be updated at the source after the select. The holdlock section of this clause is a SYBASE SQL Server reserved word that influences transaction locking. A holdlock applies only to the table or view for which it is specified, and only for the duration of the transaction defined by the statement in which it is used. While one user has taken a holdlock on a source base table, other users cannot update that table's data pages. Updates to the source base table will be delayed until the transaction that took the holdlock completes (that is, until it is committed, or until it is rolled back). Therefore, the holdlock section of this option clearly affects the consistency of the replicated data with respect to the source data during subscription materialization.

As a result of using the without holdlock option, queries at the destination Replication Server during materialization may return incomplete data for the subscription. This temporary condition ends when the create subscription command indicates that the subscription is valid. Because the replicated table may pass through states that never occurred at the source, nonatomic materialization requires that the database be set for automatic correction. Therefore, you must set autocorrection on when using without holdlock.

Do not use the without holdlock option if you update data by distributing replicated stored procedures from a source SQL Server database.

In addition, do not use the without holdlock option if you update the source data with commutative functions. For example, if a stored procedure updates a row by incrementing the previous value of a column, the value may be incorrect when materialization has completed.

The subscription materialization process for the nonatomic materialization passes through the same phases as atomic materialization.

Bulk materialization

The bulk materialization approach allows you to load source data for a subscription from media rather than pass it through the network from the source to the destination.

Here are some good reasons for using the bulk materialization approach:

- Creating the initial copy of large source datasets is computing resource-intensive, very time-consuming, and can seriously congest your computing network. Your network can get throttled because all source data rows are passed from source SQL Server to destination SQL Server, which will most likely add an unusually high packet load to the network.
- You must use the bulk materialization approach when you already have an up-to-date copy of subscription data at the destination database.

SYBASE Replication Server supports four bulk materialization methods:

1 Method 1—Subscription data is already in the destination database; in other words, you load the source data and then enable replication. If the source data already exists at the replicate site, you only have to verify that it is consistent with the source data and then define, activate, and validate subscriptions. You verify subscription consistency by using the rs_subcmp command.

2 Method 2—Suspend updates to the source table and take a snapshot of the source table.

3 Method 3—Simulate Replication Server atomic materialization.

4 Method 4—Simulate Replication Server nonatomic materialization.

Bulk materialization method 1

Here is the procedure you must follow when using the bulk materialization method 1:

1 Verify that the entire replication system is working, and take whatever steps may be necessary to make it work correctly.

2 Suspend the ability of client processes to modify the source base table.

3 Quiesce the replication system with respect to the data path from the source SQL Server to the destination SQL Server.

4 Make certain that the subscription data at destination SQL Server is identical to the source data.

5 Execute the suspend log transfer command to suspend the Log Transfer Manager for the corresponding source SQL Server database.

   5.1 Determine that there is enough free space in the source SQL Server database's transaction log to hold new log records that are created between the time the modifications to the source resume, and the time the corresponding Log Transfer Manager is resumed. Use the dbcc checktable (syslog) command to determine the amount of free space in the source database's transaction log.

6 Allow modification operations to the source data to resume.

7 Execute the define subscription command at the destination Replication Server to define the subscription you are about to materialize there.

8 Wait for subscription to be defined at both the source, and the destination, Replication Servers. Use the check subscription command to verify that the subscription is defined at both sites.
9 Execute the activate subscription command, but do not use the with suspension option to this command. This command will start the distribution of source data, and the distribution of modification database operations against the source SQL Server database, to the destination Replication Server.
10 Wait for the subscription to become active at both the source and destination sites. Use the check subscription command to verify that the subscription is active at both sites.
11 Validate the subscription at the replicate site using validate subscription command.
12 Wait for the subscription to become valid at both the source and destination sites. Use the check subscription command to verify that the subscription is validated at both sites.
13 The subscription is now materialized at the destination site.
14 Execute the resume log transfer command for the Log Transfer Manager that corresponds to the source SQL Server database transaction log.

Bulk materialization method 2

This bulk materialization method requires that you stop all applications from updating the source data. Here is the procedure you must follow when using bulk materialization method 2:

1. Verify that the entire replication system is working, and take whatever steps may be necessary to make it work correctly.
2. Suspend the ability of client processes to modify the source base table.
3. Use the admin quiesce_force_rsi command against the Replication Server(s) to quiesce Replication Server Interface threads throughout the replication system with respect to the data path from the source Replication Server to the destination Replication Server, and at any Replication Server in between.
4. Log on to the Log Transfer Manager that corresponds to the source SQL Server database's transaction log, and execute the shutdown command to shut down the Log Transfer Manager for the source database.

5 Take a table snapshot of the subscription data from the source database using a select or a database dump.

6 Once the table snapshot process completes, you can resume database operations against the SQL Server that manages the source data, providing that the corresponding Log Transfer Manager remains shut down.

6.1 Determine that there is enough free space in the source SQL Server database's transaction log to hold new log records that are created between the time of the modifications to the source resume and the time that the corresponding Log Transfer Manager is restarted.

6.2 Use the dbcc checktable (syslog) command to determine the amount of free space in the source database's transaction log.

7 Execute the define subscription command at the destination Replication Server to define the subscription you are about to materialize there.

8 Wait for subscription to be defined at both the source, and the destination, Replication Servers. Use the check subscription command to verify that the subscription is defined at both sites.

9 Execute the activate subscription command, but do not use the with suspension option to this command. This command will start the distribution of source data, and the distribution of modification database operations against the source SQL Server database, to the destination Replication Server.

10 Wait for the subscription to become active at both the source and destination sites. Use the check subscription command to verify that the subscription is active at both sites.

11 After the subscription has become active at the replicate Replication Server, suspend the Data Server Interface thread connection to the destination SQL Server database. To suspend the Data Server Interface thread, execute the suspend connection command at the destination Replication Server.

12 Execute the ltm command to restart the Log Transfer Manager that corresponds to the source SQL Server database's transaction log.

13 Begin loading the table snapshot, or database dump, into the destination SQL Server database.

While the process that loads the snapshot runs, you can continue with step 14.

14 Validate the subscription at the replicate site using the validate subscription command.

15 Wait for the subscription to become valid at both the source and destination sites. Use the check subscription command to verify that the subscription is validated at both sites.

16 When the process that loads the snapshot completes, execute the resume connection command. This will restart the Data Server Interface thread to the destination SQL Server database.

Bulk materialization method 3

Use this bulk materialization method when it is not possible to suspend updates to the source database. Here is the procedure you must follow when using bulk materialization method 3:

1 Verify that the entire replication system is working, and take whatever steps may be necessary to make it work correctly.

2 Execute the define subscription command at the destination Replication Server to define the subscription you are about to materialize there.

3 Wait for subscription to be defined at both the source, and the destination, Replication Servers. Use the check subscription command to verify that the subscription is defined at both sites.

4 After the subscription is defined, you must find its subscription ID. To find the ID of the defined subscription, log onto the Replication Server System Database at the source or destination Replication Server, and execute the following query:

```
select subid from rs_subscriptions where subname = 'NameOfSubscription'
```

5 Next, you must ensure the replicate data consistency by retrieving the subscription data, activating the subscription, and suspending the Data Server Interface thread connection to the destination SQL Server database, all in one logical unit of work against the source SQL Server database.

5.1 Begin an "open" transaction in the source SQL Server database that takes a holdlock on the base table.

5.2 Take a table snapshot of the subscription data from the source database using a select.

5.3 Execute the command rs_marker 'activate subscription SubscriptionID with suspension'.

5.4 Unlock the base table in the source SQL Server database by closing the open transaction with a commit command.

6 Wait for the subscription to become active at both the source and destination sites. Use the check subscription command to verify that the subscription is active at both sites. Even though the status of the subscription is active at the replicate Replication Server, the destination Replication Server's Data Server Interface thread for the connection to the destination SQL Server is still suspended.
7 Load the table snapshot into the destination SQL Server database.
8 Validate the subscription at the replicate site using validate subscription command.
9 Wait for the subscription to become valid at both the source and destination sites. Use the check subscription command to verify that the subscription is validated at both sites.
10 Execute the resume connection command. This will restart the Data Server Interface thread to the destination SQL Server database.

Bulk materialization method 4

Use this bulk materialization method when updates to the source database cannot be suspended and the source database data cannot be locked during the select or dump operation that retrieves the source data. This method permits a period of time during which the replicate data may be inconsistent with the source data. But, by the time the subscription becomes valid, the data should be consistent between both sites.

As previously mentioned, autocorrection must be set on during materialization so that inconsistencies resulting from continuing updates in the source database can be resolved without errors. If you distribute asynchronous procedure calls from the source SQL Server database (to modify data in the destination SQL Server database), autocorrection cannot resolve the inconsistencies, so you cannot use this bulk materialization method if your replication system also uses asynchronous procedure calls.

Here is the procedure you must follow when using the bulk materialization method 4:

1 Verify that the entire replication system is working, and take whatever steps may be necessary to make it work correctly.
2 Execute the define subscription command at the destination Replication Server to define the subscription you are about to materialize there.

3. Wait for subscription to be defined at both the source, and the destination, Replication Servers. Use the check subscription command to verify that the subscription is defined at both sites.
4. Execute the activate subscription command, using the with suspension option to this command. This command will suspend the destination Replication Server's Data Server Interface thread for the connection to the destination SQL Server.
5. Wait for the subscription to become active at both the source and destination sites. Use the check subscription command to verify that the subscription is active at both sites. Even though the status of the subscription is active at the replicate Replication Server, the destination Replication Server's Data Server Interface thread for the connection to the destination SQL Server is still suspended.
6. Take a table snapshot of the subscription data from the source database using a select or a database dump.
7. After the subscription is defined, you must find its subscription ID. To find the ID of the defined subscription, log onto the Replication Server System Database at the source or destination Replication Server, and execute the following query:

```
select subid from rs_subscriptions where subname = 'NameOfSubscription'
```

8. Execute the command rs_marker 'validate subscription SubscriptionID'.
9. Load the table snapshot into the destination SQL Server database.
10. At this point in the process, be certain to set autocorrection on for the replication definition at the destination Replication Server.
11. Execute the resume connection command. This will restart the Data Server Interface thread to the destination SQL Server database.
12. Wait for the subscription to become valid at both the source and destination sites. Use the check subscription command to verify that the subscription is validated at both sites.
13. Be certain to now set autocorrection off for replication definition at the destination Replication Server.

The procedure for replicating data

To recap this chapter, the high-level procedure for replicating data within a SYBASE replication system is as follows:

1. Cover your bases.
2. Create the replication definition.
3. Mark the source base table for replication.
4. Prepare the SYBASE accounts, and grant them the correct permissions for creating subscriptions.
5. Verify that the correct replicate table exists within the destination SQL Server database.
6. Create the subscription.

8

Replication Server functions, function calls, function strings, and function string classes

First, some definitions:

- A Replication Server function is the declaration of the name of a database operation and its associated (optional) parameter list.
- A Replication Server function call is a request that consists of the name of the function and an initialized list of data parameters. While a Replication Server function merely states what action is intended, the Replication Server function string specifies exactly how the action will be undertaken.
- A Replication Server function string class is the name of a set of all function strings used within a particular database.
- A Replication Server user-defined function is a function that you create.

Replication Server functions

Every replication system contains a suite of thirteen default system functions. Within this suite of default system functions are two main groups of functions:

1. Data manipulation functions—rs_insert; rs_update; rs_delete; rs_select; and rs_select_with_lock.
2. Database operations—All database operation system functions are implemented as stored procedures. This group is further broken into two more subgroups: transaction control directives (rs_begin; rs_commit; rs_rollback; rs_dumpdb; rs_dumptran and rs_usedb) and replication activity coordinators (rs_get_lastcommit; and rs_marker).

The data manipulation system functions are automatically created by the controlling Replication Server when a replication definition is created for an SQL Server database table. The scope of these default data manipulation system functions is limited to their replication definition. In addition, these default functions are automatically added to the default function string class rs_sql_server_function by the controlling Replication Server. These default data manipulation system functions are distributed throughout the replication system along with their replication definition.

A Replication Server function need not always be associated with a replication definition. If a function is not associated with a replication definition, then it has function string class scope. System functions that support transaction control have function string class scope.

The rs_setup_db utility automatically creates the rs_marker function when you assimilate a source SQL Server database into the replication system.

Every time a connection is created, the controlling Replication Server automatically creates the rs_begin, rs_commit, and rs_rollback transaction control directives, and the rs_get_lastcommit and rs_marker replication activity coordinators. The scope of these default system functions is limited to their function string class. Their default function string class is rs_sql_server_function. The reason why this is so is that the replication system will, by default, set the create connection's function string class parameter to the rs_sql_server_function function string class. However, you can override the default by specifying a different function string class when you execute the create connection command.

If the connection you created will initiate a coordinated database dump or coordinated transaction dump, then the rs_dumpdb and rs_dumptran system functions are automatically created for you by the controlling Replication Server. The scope of these default transaction control directives is limited to their function string class. Their default function string class is rs_sql_server_function.

Whenever the connection you create does not connect to an SQL Server database, the controlling Replication Server will not automatically create any of the data manipulation or database operation default system functions. You must create them yourself.

Data manipulation functions and function calls

The Log Transfer Manager translates scanned log records into Log Transfer Language statements. These Log Transfer Language statements are then submitted by the Log Transfer Manager to a controlling Replication Server.

The controlling Replication Server uses the rs_insert, rs_update, rs_delete, rs_begin, rs_commit, and rs_rollback system functions (and active subscription information) to:

1 Decompose the submitted Log Transfer Language statements.

2 Translate the Log Transfer Language statements into their correct function calls.

The controlling Replication Server continually maintains the integrity of its replicated data through the distribution of these function calls to destination Replication Servers. Furthermore, the format of the distributed function calls are the same regardless of who the destination data server vendor is, or the command language syntax and constructs supported by the destination data server.

A Replication Server function is the declaration of the name of a database operation its associated (optional) parameter list. By default, the Replication Server function is a request to perform a Transact-SQL command or SYBASE stored procedure call in one or more SQL Servers.

The request to perform a database operation (that is, the function) is separate from the implementation of the database operation (that is, the function string). The function merely states what action is intended, while the function string specifies exactly how the action will be undertaken.

Because the actions to be taken by the function are defined within the function's function string, it is possible to implement function strings that use language constructs other than Transact-SQL or SYBASE stored procedures. This product feature enables you to declare functions whose actions will affect non-SYBASE data servers.

Through this separation of request from method of implementation, you have the potential to:

1 Create a multivendor replication system.
2 Customize database operations on a destination database by destination database basis.

Every time a replication definition is created for a SQL Server database table, the controlling Replication Server creates a set of default data manipulation system functions specific to that particular replication definition. These default data manipulation system functions are as follows:

1 rs_insert—Used to insert a row in a destination database.
2 rs_update—Used to update a row in a destination database.
3 rs_delete—Used to delete a row in a destination database.
4 rs_select—Used to retrieve rows from a source base table when subscriptions are created or to retrieve rows from a replicate table when subscriptions are dropped.
5 rs_select_with_lock—Used to retrieve rows from a source base table when subscriptions are created or dropped, while taking a holdlock against the base source table, or to retrieve rows from a replicate table when subscriptions are dropped, while taking a holdlock against the replicate table.

The controlling Replication Server uses the active subscription information to accomplish these tasks:

1 To decompose Log Transfer Language statements.
2 To compare data values in each decomposed Log Transfer Language statement with all active subscriptions to see if a given row should be forwarded to a specific subscription site.

The controlling Replication Server will then translate these atomic Log Transfer Language statements (for which active subscriptions have been found) into function calls for each active subscription that should get the row. Log Transfer Language statements are translated into rs_insert, rs_update, or rs_delete data manipulation system function calls.

A data manipulation system function call consists of the name of the function and an initialized list of data parameters. This initialized list of data parameters will contain all required information such as the literal data values of the row columns, replication definition information, the identity of the destination data server (which may or may not be a SYBASE SQL Server), and the identity of the destination database.

When necessary, the controlling Replication Server will duplicate the atomic Log Transfer Language statements so that function calls will be distributed to each destination Replication Server that contains an active subscription. Furthermore, each duplicate function call will be transformed so that it contains the exact parameters that are correct for each specific destination Replication Server.

Each destination Replication Server that receives an rs_insert, rs_update, rs_delete, rs_begin, or rs_commit system function call, from the controlling Replication Server, will correlate that function call to a function string that will perform the intended actions against the destination database under its control. The destination Replication Server then submits the database operation to the destination data server.

At each destination site, the rs_insert, rs_update, rs_delete, rs_be gin, or rs_commit system functions will have one, and only one, function string associated with each of them. But the rs_select, and rs_ select_with_lock functions can have one or more function strings associated with each of them, at the same destination site. We will explore function strings in depth later on in this chapter.

The destination Replication Server uses the rs_select and rs_se lect_with_lock data manipulation system functions to materialize and/or dematerialize subscriptions. Because each subscription against a particular replication definition can have different predicate expressions (i.e., where clauses), the act of materializing and/or dematerializing a subscription could be different for each specific subscription. This is the reason why the rs_select and rs_select_with_lock functions can have one or more function strings associated with each of them. It is the job of the destination Replication Server to decide which rs_select or rs_select_with_lock function string to use for a particular replication definition.

Transaction control functions

The destination Replication Server must update its rs_lastcommit table whenever it receives one of the following function calls:

1 rs_commit—Commit a logical unit of work.

2 rs_dumpdb—Initiate a coordinated database dump.

3 rs_dumptran—Initiate a coordinated transaction log dump.

The destination Replication Servers Data Server Interface thread executes the rs_commit function at the end of every database operation it submits to a SQL Server database. The rs_commit updates the rs_lastcommit table by executing the rs_update_lastcommit stored procedure before the submitted database operation is committed within the destination data server. The rs_commit system function does this so that a restarted destination Replication Server will not try to resubmit a previously committed logical unit of work.

When the controlling Replication Server generates the rs_dumpdb and rs_dumptran functions, it does not generate their respective function strings. The controlling Replication Server does not generate them because of the implicit site dependencies inherent within their function strings. For example, there may well be different SYBASE devices at each participating site. Before you use these two system functions, you must create their function strings at each participating Replication Server site, and configure the Replication Server to enable it to execute coordinated dumps. Their respective function strings will execute a stored procedure that, in turn, executes the dump database and dump transaction commands. Be sure that the function strings you create also update the rs_lastcommit table. Have these function strings use the rs_update_lastcommit stored procedure to update that table. If you fail to update the rs_lastcommit table, then a participating Replication Server that has been restarted might perform a duplicate dump operation. Recall that the SQL Server does not allow the dump commands to be included in a logical unit of work that includes other Transact-SQL commands. Therefore, there is no guarantee that the dump and the update will be executed atomically.

The rs_usedb default system function changes the database context within a SQL Server. The destination Replication Servers Data Server Interface thread executes this function when it first connects to the SQL Server.

The rs_begin default system function begins a logical unit of work within an SQL Server database. The destination Replication Servers Data Server Interface thread executes this function at the start of every database operation it submits to an SQL Server database.

The rs_rollback default system function rolls back, or aborts, a logical unit of work within an SQL Server database. Aborted transactions are not currently distributed by the Replication Server; this function is currently not used.

Replication activity functions

The rs_marker replication activity function works by executing a stored procedure of the same name. The rs_marker stored procedure has been marked for replication, and is used to synchronize the subscription materialization cycle. The destination Replication Server executes the initialized rs_marker stored procedure within the source SQL Server database. The destination Replication Server uses the rs_marker stored procedure in order to pass the activate subscription and validate sub scription commands to the controlling Replication Server (the Replication Server that controls the SQL Server that manages the database that contains the source base table that the destination Replication Server is subscribing to) through the source SQL Server database's transaction log. Because it is marked for replication, the corresponding Log Transfer Manager detects the executed rs_marker stored procedure, and sends the rs_marker's @rs_api parameter (within a distribute Replication Server command) as a command to the controlling Replication Server. The ,rs_marker's @rs_api parameter contains information used by the source and destination Replication Servers to coordinate subscription materialization. The rs_marker stored procedure will only be found within Replication Servers that control a source SQL Server database.

The destination Replication Server executes the rs_get_lastcommit replication activity function when it starts a Data Server Interface thread for a destination SQL Server database. This function returns the contents of the rs_lastcommit table, which the destination Replication Server uses to find the last logical unit of work committed from each source SQL Server database. The goals of this function are to guarantee that duplicate logical units of work are not submitted to the destination SQL Server, and to guarantee that logical units of work are not overlooked.

Function strings

While a Replication Server function merely states what action is intended, the Replication Server function string specifies exactly how the action will be undertaken. Function strings are character strings that have an input template and an output template. The destination Replication Server processes these templates at runtime, resulting in a command, or stored procedure call that the destination data server is capable of executing.

Default function strings are automatically provided by destination Replication Servers for SQL Server connections that use the default SQL Server function string class, rs_sqlserver_function_class (the only exceptions to this rule are the function strings for the rs_dumpdb and the rs_dumptran functions). The default function strings are dynamically built (and rebuilt) by the destination Replication Server at runtime. The definitions of the default function strings are not stored within the destination Replication Server's Replication Server System Database. However, the definitions of custom-built function strings are stored within the destination Replication Server's Replication Server System Database, and are reused during runtime, not dynamically rebuilt.

The input and output templates are used by the destination Replication Server to locate the correct function string, or to dynamically prepare command for the destination data server. The function string class associated with the connection to the destination data server determines the language of the function strings.

As was previously explained, the rs_select and rs_select_with_lock functions can have one or more function strings associated with each of them. The input template contains a Transact-SQL select statement with a predicate expression that matches the predicate expression of a particular subscription. The destination Replication Server uses the input template to determine which one of the possible function strings is the correct function string to use. Only the rs_select and the rs_select_with_lock functions have an input template associated with them. But the rs_select function also has an output template associated with it to support the dematerialization of subscriptions from replicate tables.

The output template dictates the format of the command submitted to the destination data server. Output templates can take one of two formats:

1 Language output template—Contains a text request that the destination data server can interpret and execute. While the language request text is not interpreted by the destination Replication Server, it is parsed. The destination Replication Server maps the correct literal data values (from the function call's parameters list) to variables within the parsed language request text, and then submits the character stream to the destination data server. The language requests are implemented using the command language syntax and constructs that are supported by the destination data server.

2 Transact-SQL Remote Procedure Call output template—Contains a Transact-SQL Remote Procedure Call that the destination data server can execute, but does not interpret. The contents of the Transact-SQL Remote Procedure Call output template are parsed by the destination Replication Server, and the constructed Transact-SQL Remote Procedure Call is interpreted by the destination Replication Server. However, the Transaction-SQL Remote Procedure Call itself is not parsed by the destination Replication Server. Transact-SQL Remote Procedure Calls are usually smaller than language requests, and because they are not parsed, may consume less computing resources than language requests.

Function string classes

A Replication Server function string class is the name of a set of all function strings (both default and user-created) used within a particular database.

A specific function string class is associated with each data server connection. The default function string class for SQL Server connections is the rs_sql_server_function function string class.

It is possible for a given function string class to be associated with more than one data server connection, just so long as the function strings it contains are executable on the destination data server.

9

Transact-SQL stored procedures, replicated stored procedures, user-defined functions, and asynchronous procedure calls

First, some definitions:

- A stored procedure is an extension to the Transact-SQL language that allows you to bundle Transact-SQL commands and control-flow constructs into a named executable database object.
- A Transact-SQL stored procedure that has been marked for replication is called a replicated stored procedure.
- A user-defined function is a custom-built Replication Server function whose name and parameters are the exact match of the name and parameters of a replicated stored procedure.
- An asynchronous procedure call is produced by executing a replicated stored procedure that has been explicitly coupled to a user-defined function within the replication system.

Creating a Transact-SQL stored procedure

With stored procedures you can:

1. Combine a wide variety of Transact-SQL commands with control-of-flow constructs.
2. Define one or more parameters to be passed to the stored procedure when it is executed. You can provide a constant default value to a given parameter, which the SQL Server will use if you do not provide a value for that given parameter at the point in time when you execute the stored procedure.
3. Define one or more local variables that can be assigned literal data values within the stored procedure, while the given stored procedure is executing.
4. Define one or more values to be returned from the executed stored procedure to its caller.
5. Define return status from the executed stored procedure to its caller.
6. Execute a stored procedure on a remote SQL Server via a logical unit of work that is executing on your local SQL Server. This is referred to as making a remote procedure call. This is possible if and only if the local SQL Server and the remote SQL Server are both configured to allow remote SYBASE logins. It is important to understand that remote procedure calls are not treated as a part of the logical unit of work that is executing within the local SQL Server. If your local logical unit of work executes a remote procedure call, and then you subsequently roll back your local logical unit of work, the database operation produced on the remote SQL Server is not rolled back.
7. Execute other stored procedures from within a given stored procedure. This includes executing a stored procedure from within a trigger.
8. SYBASE users, other than the owner of the stored procedure, can be granted permission to execute a stored procedure. This permission can be granted even if the SYBASE user lacks permissions to read or modify the underlying table(s) or view(s) the stored procedure acts upon.
9. The transaction execution time is decreased (relative to Transact-SQL command statements) because a stored procedure is precompiled and its query execution plan is saved and reused whenever the stored procedure is executed. In this way the processing step to produce the query

execution plan is skipped after the first time the stored procedure runs.

10 You can explicitly instruct the SQL Server not to save the stored procedure's query execution plan, but instead to have the query execution plan generated each and every time the stored procedure is executed.

11 Place a collection of stored procedures into a given group, and destroy that collection with a single command.

12 You can create, and then use, temporary tables within a given stored procedure.

To create a Transact-SQL stored procedure, use the following command:

```
create procedure [NameOfOwner.]NameOfStoredProcedure[; number]
[[ (] @NameOfParameter SYBASEDatatype [ = default] [output]
[,@NameOfParameter SYBASEDatatype [ = default] [output]] ... [) ]] [with
   recompile]
as TransactSQLStatements
```

The name you give to the stored procedure must be unique within the SQL Server database in which it is created, and the name must conform to the rules governing SYBASE identifiers.

Executing a stored procedure in a source SQL Server

Assuming that you have the correct SQL Server database permissions, the command for executing a Transact-SQL stored procedure is as follows:

```
[execute]
NameOfSQLServer.[NameOfDatabase].[NameOfOwner].NameOfStoredProcedure
```

You can omit the execute keyword if and only if the stored procedure is the first command in a logical unit of work.

If you omit the name of the database, then the SQL Server will execute the stored procedure in the user's default database.

If you provide the name of the database, you must also provide the name of the owner of the stored procedure. There are exceptions to this rule, as follows:

1 You do not have to provide the name of the owner of the stored procedure if the person who is executing the stored procedure is also the owner of the stored procedure.

2 You do not have to provide the name of the owner of the stored procedure if the owner of the stored procedure is also the owner of the database in which it is being executed.

When a Transact-SQL stored procedure modifies a source SQL Server database table for which a replication definition exists, the following events transpire:

1 The SQL Server writes a log record, that represents the executed stored procedure, into the source database's transaction log. As is always the case, the client process that executes the database operation must not be the DB_maint_user_login account. When the DB_maint_user_login is used, the Log Transfer Manager will not forward the database operation to the destination Replication Server(s).
2 The SQL Server writes log records that represent the modifications to the source data in the source database's transaction log, and notes that these log records are marked for replication.
3 The source database transaction log's corresponding Log Transfer Manager scans the transaction log, discards the log record that represents the executed stored procedure, and forwards the log records that have been marked for replication to the controlling Replication Server.
4 After the Log Transfer Manager passes the examined log records to the controlling Replication Server, these log records follow the normal processing path for source data against which active subscriptions exist (or do not exist).
5 When the transactions eventually reach their destination SQL Server replicate databases, the Data Server Interface thread use the DB_maint_user_login account to apply the database operation(s) against the destination SQL Server replicate database.

Creating a replicated stored procedure

You create a replicated stored procedure by marking an existing Transact-SQL stored procedure for replication. To mark a Transact-SQL stored procedure for replication, use the following command:

```
sp_setreplicate NameOfTransactSQLStoredProcedure, true
```

You must ensure that the name of the replicated stored procedure is globally unique within the replication system. The Replication Server system does not ensure that the name of a replicated stored procedure is globally unique. You must manage this issue yourself.

The stored procedure that you are going to mark for replication must be defined within the source SQL Server in which it will be executed, and a local stored procedure must be defined in all SQL Server databases to which the source replicate stored procedure will be delivered. At each destination SQL Server database, the name and parameters of the local stored procedure must be identical to the source stored procedure that has been marked for replication.

It is interesting to note that the corresponding Transact-SQL stored procedure in the destination SQL Server(s) need not contain the same Transact-SQL commands and control-flow constructs as those that are found within the source replicate stored procedure. Given this product feature, you can choose to have similar or dissimilar database operations executing in the source SQL Server and in the destination SQL Server(s).

A replicated stored procedure's purpose in life is to deliver an asynchronous database operation request from one SQL Server database to other SQL Server databases within the replication system. A database operation that returns control to the calling client before waiting for the database operation to complete is referred to as an asynchronous database operation. All database operations at replicate sites are asynchronous, while database operations in source SQL Server databases may be either synchronous or asynchronous.

Executing a replicated stored procedure in a source SQL Server

When a replicated stored procedure is executed against a source SQL Server database table for which a replication definition exists, the following events occur:

1. The SQL Server writes a log record that represents the replicated stored procedure into the transaction log, and highlights the fact that it is set for replication. As is always the case, the client process that executes the database operation must not be the DB_maint_user_login account. When the DB_maint_user_login is used, the Log Transfer Manager will not forward the database operation to the destination Replication Server(s).
2. The SQL Server writes log records that represent the modifications to data rows in the source database table, and highlights the fact that they are set for replication.

3 The corresponding Log Transfer Manager scans and examines the source database's transaction log and finds the log record that represents the replicated stored procedure, and it finds the log records that represent the modifications to data rows in the source database table. Depending on the contents of the first data row's log record, the Log Transfer Manager takes one of two processing paths:

3.1 If the first data row's log record represents an update, the Log Transfer Manager packages together the replicated stored procedure and the before and after images of the data row(s), and forwards them to the controlling Replication Server.

3.2 If the first data row's log record does not represent an update, the Log Transfer Manager discards the representation of the replicated stored procedure, and forwards the data row log records in the normal manner.

4 If the first data row's log record represents an update, then the controlling Replication Server must next decompose the message the Log Transfer Manager has submitted to it, and separate the representation of the replicated stored procedure from the representation of the before and after images of the effected data row(s).

4.1 If the both the before image and the after images of the first data row match an active subscription, the replicated stored procedure's corresponding user-defined function and its initialized parameters are forwarded to the destination SQL Server(s). If the user-defined function does not exist before you execute the replicated stored procedure, then this mapping (between user-defined function and replicated stored procedure) will fail. A detailed explanation of user-defined functions will be provided shortly.

4.2 If only the before image of the first data row matches an active subscription and the after image does not, then all data rows are mapped to the default rs_delete data manipulation function. These rs_delete functions are initialized and then forwarded to the destination SQL Server(s) in the normal manner.

4.3 If only the after image of the first data row matches an active subscription, and the before image does not, than all data rows are mapped to the default rs_insert data manipulation function. These rs_insert functions are initialized and then forwarded to the destination SQL Server(s) in the normal manner.

5 When the replicated stored procedure's corresponding user-defined function and its initialized parameters arrive at the Replication Server(s) that controls the destination SQL Server(s), the connection's Data Server Interface thread maps the user-defined function to the corresponding function string. The corresponding function string contains the command to execute the corresponding stored procedure.
6 The Data Server Interface thread executes the corresponding stored procedure against the destination SQL Server database. Also, when replicated stored procedures are executed within a source SQL Server database, the SYBASE login and password of the user that initially executes the replicated stored procedure must exist at all destination SQL Server replicate databases. This is a requirement because the Data Server Interface thread will use that user's login account and password to apply the database operations against the destination SQL Server database.

When Transact-SQL stored procedures are replicated within a replication system, the potential to reduce network traffic exists because Transact-SQL stored procedures are, relative to language statements, more compact. To avoid network bottlenecks and to maintain high data transfer rates, your replication system design should keep network traffic to a minimum. Under the special conditions outlined above, only a user-defined function and its initialized parameters are forwarded to the destination SQL Server. This condition is radically different from other conditions that require the passing of the before, and/or, after images of data. The careful and considered use of a replicated stored procedure can result in significant network performance gains within replication systems where the majority of transactions being distributed are update transactions, and where subscription predicate expressions are suitable.

In addition, when replicated stored procedures are effectively used within a replication system, overall processing time (and therefore inherent replication system latency) is significantly reduced. This reduction in processing time and corresponding decrease in system latency arises because, unlike language calls, Transact-SQL stored procedure parameters are preparsed (at both the source and destination sites) before they are executed.

However, before you can put a replicate stored procedure to good use, you must create a corresponding user-defined function. When you create the corresponding user-defined function, it must take the name (and the parameters) of the replicated stored procedure upon which it is based. Once you have created the user-defined function, you will have a suite of identically named and parameterized database objects: the source replicate stored procedure, its corresponding user-defined function, and the (set of) corresponding destination stored procedure(s).

In order for this replication technique to work, all database objects in this suite must have exactly identical names and parameters. This rule may appear to violate the earlier rule that states that the name of a replicated stored procedure must be globally unique within the replication system. However, the latter rule does not violate the former rule because there is only one replicate stored procedure within the suite of identically named and parameterized database objects.

It is critically important that the replicated Transact-SQL stored procedure's parameters be exactly the same as the user-defined function, otherwise the Data Server Interface thread (that attempts to execute the Transact-SQL stored procedure) will fail. When a Data Server Interface thread fails to execute a Transact-SQL stored procedure, it automatically writes to the error log and shuts itself down.

Creating a user-defined function

User-defined functions are a type of Replication Server function. They are the type of Replication Server function that you custom-build.

Like Replication Server functions, user-defined functions have function strings, and they have a direct relationship to replication definitions:

1. A user-defined function is constructed for a specific replication definition. The scope of a user-defined function is limited to the replication definition which it corresponds to.
2. The user-defined function must be created while logged on the Replication Server where the function's replication definition was created (that is, at the Replication Server that controls the SQL Server that manages the source database tables).
3. The route between the source controlling Replication Server, and the destination controlling Replication Server must be in place before the user-defined function is created. If there are multiple destination Replication Servers, then all corresponding routes must be in place before the user-defined function is created.

However, user-defined functions also have a direct relationship to replicated stored procedures:

1. When you create a user-defined function, it takes the name and parameters of the replicated stored procedure upon which it is based. The implication of this naming relationship is that, just as the name of the replicated stored procedure is globally unique, so the name of the user-defined function is

globally unique. However, the name of the user-defined function need not be globally unique if the first parameter of the corresponding replicate stored procedure is @rs_repdef and the name of the corresponding replication definition is passed within this first parameter whenever the replicated stored procedure is executed.

2 The stored procedure must be marked for replication at the same controlling Replication Server where the corresponding user-defined function was created (that is, at controlling Replication Server where the corresponding replication definition was created).

In addition, a user-defined function has a relationship to a remote stored procedure; a stored procedure with the same name and parameters as the corresponding user-defined function must be defined in the appropriate destination SQL Server database(s).

To create a user-defined function, you log onto the controlling Replication Server and execute the following command:

```
create function
NameOfReplicationDefinition.NameOfUserDefinedFunction
([@NameOfParameter SYBASEDatatype [, @NameOfParameter SYBASEDatatype]
    ...])
```

In order to execute the create function command, you must have the create object permission granted to you for the controlling Replication Server.

When you assign a name to your user-defined function, keep in mind that the character string rs_ is reserved by the Replication Server for its own use. When creating a user-defined function, do not start a user-defined function name with the rs_ prefix. However, this restriction does not apply when you are creating the required rs_insert, rs_update, rs_delete, rs_select, rs_select_with_lock, rs_begin, rs_com mit, rs_rollback, rs_dumpdb, rs_dumptran, rs_usedb, rs_get_lastcom mit, or rs_marker functions for custom-made function string classes.

When you are designing your replication system, bear in mind that you will have to use user-defined function if:

1 Replicated stored procedures are to be executed in a source SQL Server database that is under the control of a Replication Server.

2 You want to request a database operation at the source SQL Server database, from within a destination replicate SQL Server database.

3 You want to replicate stored procedures from the source SQL Server database to destination replicate SQL Server databases, instead of using Transact-SQL language commands.

Creating the function string for the user-defined function

Like Replication Server functions, user-defined functions have a direct relationship to function strings:

1. A user-defined function has a corresponding function string.
2. The user-defined function must exist before you create its function string.

Function string classes are associated with specific SQL Server database connections. When a connection is created, the rs_sqlserver_function_class function string class is associated with it, by default. Default function strings are automatically provided by destination Replication Servers for SQL Server connections that use the default SQL Server function string class. The default function strings are dynamically built by the destination Replication Server during runtime.

When you create a user-defined function, the Replication Server creates, for all connections that use the default rs_sqlserver_function_class function string class, the corresponding function string. This default function string will execute a stored procedure with the same name and parameters as the user-defined function. However, you must create the stored procedure in the destination SQL Server database(s) where the user-defined function call will be distributed to. Another option is available to you though; you can create a custom-built function string for your user-defined function.

To create a custom-built function string, log onto the Replication Server that controls the destination SQL Server database, and execute the following command:

```
create function string
[NameOfReplicationDefinition.]NameOfFunction [;NameOfInstance]
for NameOfFunctionStringClass
[scan 'InputTemplateCharacterString'
[output {language 'OutputTemplateCharacterString' |
rpc 'execute NameOfTransactSQLStoredProcedure
[@NameOfParameter =] {constant | ?variable!mod?}
[@NameOfParameter =] {constant | ?variable!mod?}] ...'}]
```

To execute the create function string command, you must have create object permission on the Replication Server that controls the destination SQL Server database.

The instance name is the optional name of the function string. By default, a function string takes the name of the Replication Server function for which it is created. The name of the function string must conform to the SYBASE rules for identifiers. If you elect to assign a name to the function string you have created, keep in mind that the character string rs_ is reserved by the Replication Server for its own use. When creating a user-defined function, do not start a user-defined function name with the rs_ prefix. However, this restriction does not apply when you are creating function strings that support the required user-defined functions for custom-made function string classes (that is, for the rs_insert, rs_update, rs_delete, rs_select, rs_select_with_lock, rs_begin, rs_commit, rs_rollback, rs_dumpdb, rs_dumptran, rs_usedb, rs_get_lastcommit, or rs_marker functions).

It is extremely important, when declaring the function string's stored procedure, that the listed parameters appear exactly as they do in the destination SQL Server database's stored procedure. Recall that even though a function string's remote Transact-SQL stored procedure call type output template is parsed, the Replication Server does not check the output template's parameters against those:

1. In the corresponding user-defined function.
2. In the corresponding replication definition.
3. In the corresponding replicated stored procedure.
4. Transact-SQL stored procedures contained within the function string.

For that matter, parameters are not checked when language construct type output templates are used either. More importantly, errors in specifying parameters will not appear until the Replication Server tries to apply the transactions using function strings. If errors occur at that point, the Data Server Interface thread will log the error and will then shut itself down.

Asynchronous procedure call

An asynchronous procedure call is the execution of a replicated Transact-SQL stored procedure in one SQL Server database that is then distributed by the replication system to be executed at another SQL Server database. The Replication Server that manages the site at which the asynchronous procedure call originates maps the replicate stored procedure to a replication definition via a corresponding user-defined function, and distributes the asynchronous procedure call back to the source site(s).

If an asynchronous procedure call is invoked within a replicate SQL Server database, then that replicate SQL Server database must have a corresponding Log Transfer Manager. And, in addition to the route that exists from the Replication Server that controls the source SQL Server database, to the Replication Server that controls the destination

SQL Server replicate database, there must exist another route from the destination Replication Server to the source Replication Server.

Typically, asynchronous procedure calls are invoked within a replicate SQL Server database for distribution back to the source SQL Server database. As such, the replicate SQL Server database has subscriptions to the source SQL Server database. The replicate stored procedure that executes within the replicate database must not directly modify the replicate data, and it need not modify real production data at all. The replicate stored procedure that executes within the replicate database need only update a dummy table so that the execution of the replicated stored procedure can be recorded in the replicate SQL Server database's transaction log so that it is scanned, examined and forwarded by a Log Transfer Manager to the Replication Server (that controls the replicate SQL Server database) for distribution back to the source SQL Server database. When the corresponding user-defined function is applied to the source SQL Server database, the controlling Replication Server's Data Server Interface thread uses the SYBASE login and password of the user that invoked the asynchronous procedure call when applying the corresponding database operation to the source SQL Server database. The modifications to the source SQL Server database will be handled in the usual fashion. That is, the source SQL Server database's Log Transfer Manager will scan, examine, and forward the modified data rows to the source SQL Server's controlling Replication Server. The controlling Replication Server will distribute the modified data rows to all subscribing sites. The destination Replication Server's Data Server Interface thread will, as the DB_maint_user_login account, apply the corresponding database operation to destination SQL Server replicate database. In this way, database operations that initiate within a replicate database can indirectly modify source data.

The design of a replication system that makes asynchronous procedure calls at replicate sites is an extremely complex topic. A world of new and complex replication system design variations opens up to you when you incorporate the use of asynchronous procedure calls into your replication system design. For a detailed, in-depth discussion of designing and implementing replication system designs that use asynchronous procedure calls, refer to appendix B's "Global Online Transaction Replication System" case study.

10

Replication system security

So far I have explored in depth the components and language constructs that make up a replication system. Now I will explore replication system security matters relating to "authorized" users that represent such a risk exposure within a replication system.

Authorized users

The list of *authorized* SYBASE SQL Server accounts within a replication system would include:

1. SQL Server sa accounts at all primary and replicate database sites. The corresponding Log Transfer Manager will, by default, use the SYBASE login of the database owner to gain access to the database's transaction log. However, if you do not include the name of the owner of the SQL Server database, then the Log Transfer Manager will use the managing SQL Server's sa login.
2. SYBASE accounts that own primary or replicate databases under the control of the replication system. The corresponding Log Transfer Manager will, by default, use this login to gain access to the database's transaction log.
3. SYBASE accounts that own tables and stored procedures that have been marked for replication within, or that indirectly support, primary and replicate databases.

The list of authorized Replication Server accounts within a replication system would include:

1. SYBASE accounts that are permitted to create replication definitions.
2. SYBASE accounts that are permitted to create subscriptions.

3 SYBASE accounts that are permitted to mark tables and stored procedures for replication.
4 SYBASE accounts that are permitted to create user-defined functions.
5 SYBASE accounts that are permitted to create function strings.
6 SYBASE accounts that are permitted to execute replicated stored procedures.

The list of authorized administration Replication Server accounts within a replication system would include:

1 The ID Server login name (ID_Server_user) that other Replication Servers will use to connect to the ID Server.
2 The Replication Server's sa login.
3 The SYBASE login name (DB_Maint_user) that the controlling Replication Server will use when updating replicated data within the SQL Server database.
4 The SYBASE login name (LTM_RS_user) of a controlling Replication Server user account that Log Transfer Manager will use to log into the controlling Replication Server.
5 The SYBASE login name (LTM_admin_user) for the user who will start up and shut down this particular Log Transfer Manager.
6 The SYBASE login name (RSSD_prim_user) of the primary user of the Replication Server System database. Replication Servers use the RSSD_prim_user login name and password for Replication Server System Database updates that are replicated to other sites, such as those related to replication definitions.
7 The SYBASE login name (RSSD_maint_user) of the maintenance user of the Replication Server System database. Replication Servers use the RSSD_maint_user login name and password for RSSD updates that are not replicated to other sites, such as those related to rejected transactions.
8 The SYBASE login name (RSSD_DBO_user) of the database owner of the Replication Server System database.
9 The SYBASE login name (RS_RS_user) that other Replication Servers will use to connect to a given Replication Server.

The list of authorized UNIX users within a replication system would include:

1 UNIX accounts that have write or delete permissions to the interfaces file(s) for the replication system processes.
2 UNIX accounts that have write or delete permissions to the database setup parameters file(s). As these database setup files contain SYBASE login names and their passwords, it is

critically important the count of authorized UNIX accounts be held to a minimum.

3 UNIX accounts that have write or delete permission to the Replication Server installation file(s). As these Replication Server installation files contain SYBASE login names and their passwords, it is critically important that the count of authorized UNIX accounts be held to a minimum.

SYBASE login account passwords

As the Log Transfer Manager will, by default, use this SYBASE login name and password to gain access to the database's transaction log, the database owner's password cannot be changed as in the past. For as long as the database is assimilated into the replication system, you must synchronize the change in the database owner's password with the corresponding Log Transfer Manager.

As a Log Transfer Manager may use the SQL Server sa login and password to gain access to a source database's transaction log, the SQL Server sa's password cannot be changed as in the past. If you are not providing the Log Transfer Manager with the SYBASE database owner login, then you must synchronize the change in the SQL Server sa login's password with all corresponding Log Transfer Managers.

Any SYBASE account that is permitted to execute replicated stored procedures cannot have its password changed as in the past. When one of these accounts changes its password, then at all sites to which the replicated stored procedure is distributed, the password of this account at all destination SQL Servers must be changed simultaneously.

When you change the password of the ID_Server_user login, be sure to change it at all Replication Servers within the ID Server's domain.

When you change the password of the RS_RS_user, be sure to change it at all Replication Servers that have a route to that particular Replication Server.

Database object permissions

Be sure to grant authorized SYBASE login accounts the required permission to execute replicated stored procedures at all sites where the corresponding Transact-SQL stored procedure exists.

It is recommended that the permission to update, insert or delete data in replicated tables be restricted to the corresponding DB_Maint_user account. If you allow any other accounts to modify the contents of a replicate table, then consistency between the source and replicate database will be up for grabs.

Replication Server maintenance user permissions

The rs_setup_db utility creates the SYBASE login name of the maintenance user that the controlling Replication Server will use when updating replicated data within a given SQL Server database. However, the rs_setup_db utility does not grant the correct database permissions, to the maintenance user, on the tables that will hold replicated data.

For each table in the destination database that will hold replicate data, you must grant the controlling Replication Server's maintenance user SYBASE login account the permission to insert, update, and delete all tables that will hold replicate data.

Also, the controlling Replication Server uses the maintenance user SYBASE login to the destination database to maintain its rs_lastcommit table. It is up to you to ensure that the controlling Replication Server maintenance account has permission to execute the destination database's rs_update_lastcommit and rs_get_lastcommit stored procedures.

Replication definition permissions

The intention of the optional searchable columns clause is to restrict the variety of subscriptions that can be written against a particular replication definition. If you do not use the optional searchable columns clause, then all subscriptions against a particular replication definition must be for all columns contained within that particular replication definition. If you use the optional searchable columns clause, then the predicate expression (the where clause), of all subscriptions you create against this particular replication definition, can only refer to the searchable column(s).

Subscriptions permissions

Because of the confidential nature of most business data, and because of the resource intensive nature of subscription materialization, it is recommended that only a minimal number of SYBASE accounts be authorized to create subscriptions.

Here are the various accounts and permissions that have to be established before you can create or define a subscription:

1 You must have the same login account and password at the destination Replication Server, at the Replication Server that controls the source, and at the SQL Server that manages the source database.
2 Your SYBASE login account must have been added to the source database.
3 At the destination Replication Server, where the create subscription command will execute, you must have at least create object permission.
4 At the source Replication Server, you must have create object permission, or at least primary subscribe permission.
5 In the source database, your SYBASE login account must have select permission on the source base table.
6 A user creating a subscription must have execute permission on rs_marker in the source SQL Server database. The rs_marker system function and stored procedure provides the Replication Server with a means to support subscription materialization.
7 The Replication Server maintenance user for the replicate database must have update, delete, insert, and select permission on the replicate table.

Replicate stored procedure permissions

When a user executes a replicate stored procedure in one SQL Server, their SYBASE login account and password must exist at all sites where the replicate stored procedure will be distributed to. The reason why this is so is that the destination Replication Server's Data Server Interface will use the originating user's SYBASE login account and password to apply the database operation.

In addtion, the user's SYBASE login account that originated the replicate stored procedure must have permissions to execute the rs_update_lastcommit system function, and permission to update the rs_lastcommit table at the destination Replication Server(s).

Rather than granting execute permissions to public for the rs_update_lastcommit Transact-SQL stored procedure, it is recommended that you restrict the permission to the user SYBASE login accounts that are allowed to create subscriptions, that are allowed to execute replicated stored procedures, or that are allowed to execute asynchronous procedure calls.

Log transfer manager permissions

It is possible to interactively submit Log Transfer Language statements to the Replication Server. Therefore, do not create any SYBASE account other than the default account that is authorized to log onto the Log Transfer Manager.

11

Recovering a replication system

There are far too many possible ways by which a replication system can fail, in part or whole, to document. The intention of this chapter is to help you develop your troubleshooting skills and to present the main techniques for recovering individual replication system components.

The myth of high availability

Increasing the number of SQL Servers from which business information is available to your organization through the application of data replication techniques and technologies does not constitute high availability.

When you examine a technology's claim of high availability, you need to consider its *mean time between failures* and its *mean time to repair*. And, when you consider a data replication technology's claims to high availability, you must include, within its mean time to repair aspect, the time it takes to recover the integrity of a distributed database. Remember, the end user will not perceive the replication system as having been recovered if his or her database lacks integrity.

The SYBASE Replication Server does absolutely nothing to reduce mean time between failures. To the contrary, by introducing more nodes into your system configuration (that is, you add in one or more Replication Servers, one or more Log Transfer Managers, etc.) you directly increase the chance of a node failure event within your system. And, as the number of nodes increases, the mean time to repair will, in all likelihood, also increase.

The SYBASE Replication Server does absolutely nothing to decrease mean time to repair. It is prudent to state that, once you understand the complex heuristics of recovering the integrity of a replication system, the mean time to repair will increase significantly. In the case of a SYBASE replication system, the recovery heuristics can be very complex and are more often than not labor intensive, with only moderate automatic failure management. You need to accept the fact that you will not be able to bounce your replication system back quickly.

Another way of looking at this myth of high availability is to take the position that any node on the distributed high availability computing system is capable of taking over any other node on the system that fails. This is the viewpoint that embraces the notions of hot, warm, and cool backup nodes. For the sake of discussion, let's qualify a hot backup as a node that can take over in under a minute, a warm backup node is one that can take over in under five minutes, and a cool backup is a node that can eventually take over.

A high availability client/server system needs to provide an automated transaction failure management facility to handle active client processes. While the SQL Server does have automated open transaction failure management facilities, the Replication Server and Log Transfer Manager do not.

The SYBASE Replication Server is not capable of redirecting active client processes from their current SQL Server to any other alternate SQL Server in the event that their current SQL Server fails.

Recall that the SYBASE Replication Server is limited by the hard demarcation of source data vs. replicate data. Let's consider just a few of the many time-consuming tasks you will have to handle in the event that the current data source/sink crashes. First, you will have to ensure that the replication system has forwarded and applied all committed transactions to the backup. You have to intervene manually to redress the issue of any failed open transactions. Once these two processes have completed successfully, you will have to execute all of the replication definitions (create all stored procedures, replicated stored procedures, user-defined functions, function strings, and function string classes) for the backup site, and will have to handle the subscriptions at all destination sites. Let's assume that you have previously ensured that all user accounts, passwords, and database object permissions at the backup are exactly in sync with the crashed primary site, as well as any site that will be applying remote procedures against the backup. As you can imagine, while you are off doing all of this absolutely necessary housekeeping, merciless time has continued to move forward, and you are still not yet certain of the relationship between active client processes and the integrity of the backup database.

So, as you can see, between the point in time when the client process's primary site fails, and the point in time when the client process begins to modify the backup database, the backup site has lost a lot of its thermal mass. However, your end users may have probably gotten a bit hot under the collar while they had to wait for the replication system to come back on line. So, in order to effectively manage the expectations of your end users, be sure not to present the SYBASE Replication Server system to them as anything more than a component within a computing system that has cool backups. The SYBASE Replication Server is but one of the tools you will need to deploy in order to provide your business with a cool backup. And, be prepared to roll a lot of your own code to automate transaction failure management.

A source SQL Server crashes

When a source SQL Server crashes, you need to be on the lookout for orphaned open transactions. An open transaction is a transaction for which a commit or roll back command has not yet been associated. An orphaned open transaction is an open transaction on an inbound stable queue that will never have (for a number of reasons we will explore later in this chapter) a commit or roll back command associated with it. In the event that an open transaction is orphaned within the Replication Server, you are required to purge that transaction.

There are two things to consider when handling orphaned transactions. First, the Log Transfer Manager can, for a given scan, write a combination of completed and orphaned transactions onto the inbound stable queue. Secondly, only by purging the orphaned transaction(s) will any succeeding completed transaction(s) work their way through the Replication Server(s) and eventually out to your backup server(s).

Bear in mind that "open" is a relative term here. The transaction may have completed within the SQL Server, but the Log Transfer Manager may not have scanned the commit or roll back log records associated with this transaction. So the same transaction can be completed relative to the SQL Server, and open relative to the replication system.

In this case, if you are unable to recover the source SQL Server database, or if you decide to use a backup server, the SYBASE Replication Server does not provide you with a way to recover the open orphaned transaction. You have to address the issues of lost database integrity due to orphaned transactions.

Once you purge the orphaned transaction, any and all completed transactions written behind it on the inbound stable queue will automatically be processed and applied to all destination SQL Server databases. Once that happens, you have to be concerned with the consequences of the loss of transaction integrity within the replication system. You have to address the issues of lost database integrity due to a loss of transaction integrity.

However, if the source SQL Server database is capable of being recovered without any loss of integrity (that is, you do not use any of the ways of recovering the crashed database that do not ensure database integrity), then the Log Transfer Manager will scan the transaction log and pick up the associated commit or roll back log records, and the open transaction will not become orphaned but will instead complete.

When things go wrong with the Log Transfer Manager

Every SQL Server database that is the source of data or stored procedures requires a Log Transfer Manager. As we know, the Log Transfer Manager maintains a secondary truncation point within the SQL Server database's transaction log. Periodically, the Log Transfer Manager updates this secondary truncation point to reflect transactions passed to the controlling Replication Server.

The SQL Server maintains its own primary truncation point within the transaction log. Under normal conditions the SQL Server cannot advance its primary truncation point past the Log Transfer Manager's secondary truncation point. If the controlling Replication Server is down for a long time, the Log Transfer Manager is unable to read records from the transaction log, and is unable to update the secondary truncation point location, thereby preventing the SQL Server from truncating the transaction log past the log record referenced by the Log Transfer Manager's secondary truncation point.

There is a way to advance the SQL Server's primary truncation point under this scenario, but doing so may well destroy the integrity of the transactions being distributed.

Turning off a log truncation point in an SQL Server source database

Turning off a Log Transfer Manager's secondary truncation point should be avoided if at all possible. However, if the source SQL

Server is running out of free transaction log space, then you may have to turn off the Log Transfer Manager's secondary truncation point.

The first thing to do is to ensure that the SQL Server source database is incapable of continuing to forward transactions. To accomplish this, log onto the Replication Server that controls the SQL Server that manages the source database, and, as the Replication Server sa, execute the following command:

```
suspend log transfer from NameOfSQLServer.NameOfDatabase
go
```

The suspend log transfer command will disconnect the corresponding Log Transfer Manager from the controlling Replication Server, and will prevent the corresponding Log Transfer Manager from reconnecting to the controlling Replication Server. At this point in time, the source SQL Server database is incapable of having its transactions distributed.

Next, you need to turn off the Log Transfer Manager's secondary truncation point in the source SQL Server database. To do this, log onto the SQL Server that manages the source database, and, as the SQL Server sa or as the database owner login, execute the following commands:

```
use NameOfDatabase
go
dbcc settrunc (ltm, ignore)
go
```

Once this command completes, the source SQL Server will be able to advance its primary truncation point past the Log Transfer Manager's secondary truncation point, and the Log Transfer Manager has been suspended. You may now shut down the Log Transfer Manager.

If the source SQL Server database's transaction log is truncated while the corresponding Log Transfer Manager is suspended, then the following problems may occur:

1. Orphaned transactions exist.
2. The replication system has lost its transaction integrity.
3. Subscription materialization commands against the source database that are lost or interrupted require manual clean-up of the subscription materialization stable queues and replicate tables, and a reissuance of the affected subscription commands.

Restarting a suspended Log Transfer Manager

Before starting a suspended Log Transfer Manager, you have to reestablish the Log Transfer Manager's secondary truncation point within the source SQL Server database. To do this, log onto the SQL Server that manages the source database, and, as the SQL Server sa or as the database owner, execute the following command:

```
use NameOfDatabase
go
dbcc settrunc (ltm, valid)
go
```

The ltm_trunc_state column in the output reported by the dbcc settrunc command should contain a 1, indicating that the Log Transfer Manager's secondary truncation point has been reestablished. However, the value of locater (this is an internal system table attribute that tells the Log Transfer Manager to begin scanning the source database's transaction log) is incorrect. So, you must now reset the literal data value of locater by executing the command:

```
update rs_locator set locater = 0x0
where sender = (select dbid from rs_databases
where dsname = 'NameOfSQLServer'
and dbname = 'NameOfDatabase')
and type = 'E'
go
```

Any previous suspend log transfer command would have disconnected the Log Transfer Manager from the controlling Replication Server. To reconnect the Log Transfer Manager to the controlling Replication Server, log onto the controlling Replication Server and, as the Replication Server sa, execute the following command:

```
resume log transfer from NameOfSQLServer.NameOfDatabase
go
```

Following the successful execution of the above command, you may restart the Log Transfer Manager if required.

If the SQL Server transaction log was truncated while the Log Transfer Manager was suspended, significant inconsistencies within the replication system can exist.

Troubleshooting a Log Transfer Manager failure

Errors can occur within a Log Transfer Manager while it is in the process of transferring transactions from the source SQL Server database transaction log. These errors may originate from:

1 The SQL Server that manages the source database.
2 The controlling Replication Server.
3 The Log Transfer Manager.

The Log Transfer Manager records error numbers and error messages in its error log. When starting the Log Transfer Manager, the identity of the operating system file that is its error log is specified with the -E command-line option. The error messages indicate which server caused the error so that you can troubleshoot the Log Transfer Manager failure. But, unlike Replication Server error actions, Log Transfer Manager error actions are not user-configurable.

When examining the contents of the Log Transfer Manager's error log, the literal data values of the number of SQL Server errors, related to scanning the source database's transaction log, are between 9100 and 9199.

Problems with starting a Log Transfer Manager

At startup, the Log Transfer Manager attempts to log onto the corresponding SQL Server by establishing an Open Client connection, using the SQL Server sa login name and password or the source database owner's login name and password. As usual, if either login name or password is invalid, then the connection attempt will fail.

Also, at startup, the Log Transfer Manager attempts to log in to the Replication Server by establishing an Open Client connection, using a specific login name and password. If that login name or password is invalid, or if that specific login name does not have connect source permission, then the connection attempt will fail.

After successfully establishing the Open Client connection to the SQL Server, the Log Transfer Manager executes the dbcc settrunc command on the SQL Server to set the Log Transfer Manager truncation point. During startup, the Log Transfer Manager looks up the literal data value of locater (within the rs_locater table in the

Replication Server System Database) to determine where to begin scanning the database transaction log. If, when executing the dbcc settrunc command, the Log Transfer Manager specifies an invalid truncation page to the SQL Server, an error is recorded and the Log Transfer Manager terminates. You should expect this type of error whenever the source database's transaction log has been truncated after one has set its truncation state to "ignore."

If a Log Transfer Manager is restarted during the period of time that the Log Transfer Manager's log scan thread is sleeping (Log Transfer Manager configuration parameter scan_retry), the source SQL Server will reject the Log Transfer Manager connection because the sleeping log scan thread has not released the previous Log Transfer Manager connection. When the thread wakes up, the SQL Server will release the previous connection and then accept the new Log Transfer Manager connection.

When a Log Transfer Manager restarts, it may resend some log records that the Replication Server has already processed. If the Replication Server receives a record with a lower origin queue ID (oqid) than the last record it processed, it assumes the record is a duplicate and ignores it.

Log Transfer Manager fatal errors

Whenever a fatal error occurs, the Log Transfer Manager disconnects from the SQL Server and Replication Server and terminates. When the Log Transfer Manager terminates, it may leave the SQL Server or the Replication Server in a state where things are not cleaned up, and the server may believe the terminated Log Transfer Manager is still connected. This errant connection is called a *phantom* connection.

To get around the errant connection problem, it is necessary to shut down and restart the Replication Server.

Problems with stable queues

There are three basic problems relating to Replication Server stable queues:

1 Depletion of free space
2 Failed subscription materialization
3 A stable queue contains a corrupted message

Disk partition utilization

In order to determine if you do or if you do not have free disk space, you need to determine the utilization of all disk partitions for a given Replication Server. To display the utilization of all disk partitions being used by a given Replication Server, log onto that particular Replication Server (as any user), and execute this command:

```
admin disk_space
go
```

The output of the admin disk_space command will tell you, on a per-partition basis, the total number of segments on the partition and the total number of segments currently in use by the given Replication Server.

If you have run out of free stable queue space, and you have free disk drive partitions, then start an isql session and add a new partition.

Collecting information about stable queues

In order to dump a stable queue, you must know the identity of the starting segment, the identity of the block in the segment where the dump is to begin, and the number of the blocks to be dumped. To find the data values of the identity of the starting segment, the identity of the block in the segment where the dump is to begin, you must examine the threads within the Replication Server. To accomplish that task, log onto the particular Replication Server and, as any user, execute this command:

```
admin who
go
```

Information about all threads will be displayed. The information of main interest is in the Spid and the Info fields. The Spid is a unique identifier for the Stable Queue Manager thread. If a given thread is suspended or down, this field is left blank. The Info field contains three subfields, the stable queue number (q_number), the stable queue type (q_type) and the stable queue identifier. The contents of the Info field subfields are dependent upon the type of thread it represents.

For Stable Queue Manager threads and for Stable Queue Transaction Interface threads, the contents of the Info field subfields are as follows:

1. q_number—Contains the numeric identifier of the Replication Server, or SQL Server database, site.
2. q_type—Contains a 1 for an inbound stable queue, a 0 for an outbound stable queue; any other number is the identifier for a subscription materialization stable queue.
3. stable queue identifier—For subscription materialization stable queues, it contains the name of the corresponding replication definition and the name of the associated subscription. For outbound queues to other Replication Servers, it contains the name of the other Replication Server. For outbound queues to SQL Server databases, it contains the name of the SQL Server. And, for inbound queues of Log Transfer Managers, it contains the name of the SQL Server database.

If you want this same information for just the Replication Server's Stable Queue Manager threads, then log on to the particular Replication Server, and as any user, execute this command:

```
admin who,sqm
go
```

Between the point in time when you produce the admin who,sqm report on a Stable Queue Manager thread and the point in time when you dump a particular stable queue, the Stable Queue Manager thread may have been actively adding and deleting message blocks and segments from the stable queues. So by the point in time when you run the sysadmin dump_queue command, the output of the admin who,sqm command may no longer be accurate. To prevent degradation in the quality of the admin who,sqm command output, you should place the Replication Server in stand-alone mode or suspend database connections or routes prior to executing the admin who,sqm command.

If you want this same information for just the Replication Server's Stable Queue Transaction Interface threads, then log onto the particular Replication Server, and as any user, execute this command:

```
admin who,sqt
go
```

For Log Transfer Manager User or Executor threads, the contents of the Info field subfields are as follows:

1. q_number—Contains the numeric identifier of the Replication Server, or SQL Server database, site.
2. q_type—Contains a 1 for an inbound stable queue, a 0 for an outbound stable queue; any other number is the identifier for a subscription materialization stable queue.
3. stable queue identifier—The name of the corresponding source SQL Server, and the name of the corresponding source SQL Server database.

For Replication Server Interface threads, the Info field contains the name of the Replication Server to which messages are being sent. If you want this same information for just the Replication Server's Replication Server Interface threads, then log onto the particular Replication Server and, as any user, execute this command:

```
admin who,rsi
go
```

For Data Server Interface threads, the Info field contains the name of the SQL Server to which messages are being submitted. If you want this same information for just the Replication Server's Data Server Interface threads, then log onto the particular Replication Server, and as any user, execute this command:

```
admin who,dsi
go
```

For Distributor threads, the contents of the Info field subfields are as follows:

1. q_number—Contains the numeric identifier of the Replication Server, or SQL Server database, site.
2. q_type—Contains a 1 for an inbound stable queue, a 0 for an outbound stable queue; any other number is the identifier for a subscription materialization stable queue.
3. stable queue identifier—The name of the corresponding source SQL Server, and the name of the corresponding source SQL Server database whose transactions it is distributing.

Failed subscription materialization

Sometimes the Replication Server will encounter an unrecoverable error while materializing a subscription. If this failure event arises, you will have to stop and delete the subscription materialization stable queue. Before you can stop and delete the failed subscription materialization stable queue, you need to determine its identifier and type. To delete a subscription materialization stable queue, log on to that particular Replication Server, and as the Replication Server's sa account, execute this command:

```
sysadmin drop_queue, NumberOfStableQueue, StableQueueType
go
```

NumberOfStableQueue is the site identifier of the Replication Server or SQL Server database that is the source, or destination, for the subscription materialization stable queue. *StableQueueType* is the type of the stable queue. Do not use this command for any other purpose than to stop and delete a subscription materialization stable queue!

Troubles in stable queue land

If you suspect that a stable queue may contain a corrupt message or messages, you will have to examine the contents of that stable queue. However, stable queues have to be dumped before their contents can be examined. Note that a dump of the contents of the stable queue does not purge the stable queue of its contents.

The dump of a stable queue can be sent to:

1 System tables within the Replication Server System Database. If the contents of a stable queue are dumped into the Replication Server System Database, then the target system tables are cleared of any existing messages that have the same identifier, type, segment ID, and block ID as the blocks being dumped.
2 The default Replication Server log.
3 An alternate dump file. There is another utility that uses the dump file, so it is advisable to isolate specific dump events to specific alternate dump file targets. As to be expected, the current dump file is closed whenever a new dump file is opened.

Before you attempt to dump the contents of a particular stable queue, be certain to place the respective Replication Server in standalone mode, or suspend all database connections and routes associated with that Replication Server.

Dumping the contents of a stable queue

To dump the contents of a particular stable queue to an alternative log file, you have to first specify the operating system file to use. To specify the alternative log file, log onto that particular Replication Server, and, as the Replication Server sa, execute the following command:

```
sysadmin dump_file NameOfOperatingSystemFile
go
```

In order to close the existing dump file, execute, as the sa user, the command:

```
sysadmin dump_file
go
```

This closes the current file, without opening a new file. It is probably a good idea to close the current dump file, but keep in mind that the default dump file is the Replication Server log.

Now, when you execute the sysadmin dump_queue command, and do not set the optional RSSD flag, the contents of the stable queue will be written to the identified operating system file.

To dump the contents of a particular stable queue to the Replication Server's log file, log onto the Replication Server as the Replication Server sa and execute this command:

```
sysadmin dump_queue, NumberOfStableQueue, StableQueueType,
IdentityOfStartingSegment, IdentityOfStartingBlock, NumberOfBlocksToDump
go
```

The Replication Server will recognize four special literal data values for the *IdentityOfStartingSegment* and *IdentityOfStartingBlock* parameters of the sysadmin dump_queue command:

1 If the literal data value of the *IdentityOfStartingSegment* parameter equals –1, then the dump will start with the first active segment in the stable queue.

2 If the literal data value of the *IdentityOfStartingSegment* parameter equals –2, then the dump will start with the first segment in the stable queue, including all inactive segments in the stable queue. Inactive segments are retained within a stable queue in accordance with the established save interval.

3 If the literal data value of the *IdentityOfStartingSegment* parameter equals –1 and the literal data value of the *IdentityOfStartingBlock* parameter equals –1, then the dump will start with the first undeleted block in the stable queue.

4 If the literal data value of the *IdentityOfStartingSegment* parameter equals –1 and the literal data value of the *IdentityOfStartingBlock* parameter equals –2, then the dump will start with the first unread block in the stable queue.

To force the dump of the stable queue to system tables within the Replication Server System Database, set the sysadmin dump_queue command's optional flag as follows:

```
sysadmin dump_queue, NumberOfStableQueue, StableQueueType,
IdentityOfStartingSegment, IdentityOfStartingBlock, NumberOfBlocksToDump,
   RSSD
go
```

The technique of dumping a stable queue to tables within the Replication Server System Database has, compared to the other two dump targets, the worst level of performance. This poor level of performance is due to the incursion of internal SQL Server processing overhead within this particular dump technique. However, by dumping the messages into the Replication Server System Database, you can execute SQL queries against the messages dumped from the stable queue. Just be sure to determine that there is enough disk space available within the Replication Server System Database to store the dumped messages.

Examining the contents of a Stable Queue Transaction Interface thread transaction cache

Every Stable Queue Transaction Interface thread has a dedicated volatile memory cache where it stores transactions it is currently processing (on behalf of a Distributor thread, or on behalf of a Data Server Interface thread). This dedicated volatile memory cache is called a Stable Queue Transaction Interface Transaction Cache. The size of the Stable Queue Transaction Interface Transaction Cache is a tunable Replication Server parameter (sqt_max_cache_size).

In order to examine the contents of a given Stable Queue Transaction Interface Transaction Cache, its contents must be dumped. Before you can dump the contents of a Stable Queue Transaction Interface Transaction Cache, you must get information about the identity of the cache. To get the information you will need, log onto the particular Replication Server, and as any user, execute this command:

```
admin who,sqt
go
```

Information about the Stable Queue Transaction Interface threads, and the transactions they are currently processing, will be displayed. The information of main interest is the Spid and the Info fields. The Spid is a unique identifier for the Stable Queue Transaction Interface thread. If a Stable Queue Transaction Interface thread is suspended or down, this field is left blank. The Info field contains three subfields; the queue number (q_number), the queue type (q_type), and the queue identifier. In order to dump the contents of a Transaction Cache, its q_number and q_type must be known.

The dump of the stable queue can be sent to:

- the Replication Server log
- an alternate dump file

In order to dump only open transactions in the Stable Queue Transaction Interface Transaction Cache, log onto the Replication Server and execute, as the sa user, the command:

```
sysadmin sqt_dump_queue, NumberOfStableQueue,
StableQueueType, open
go
```

In order to dump all transactions in the Stable Queue Transaction Interface Transaction Cache, log onto the Replication Server and execute, as the sa user, the command:

```
sysadmin sqt_dump_queue, NumberOfStableQueue,
StableQueueType
go
```

Purging open transactions from inbound stable queues

The Replication Server provides two commands for purging open transactions from inbound stable queues:

1. sysadmin purge_first_open—Purges only the first open transaction from a particular inbound stable queue.
2. sysadmin purge_all_open—Purges all open transactions from a particular inbound stable queue.

These commands can only be used on inbound stable queues. In addition, the Replication Server needs free stable queue space to purge the open transactions.

If you want to examine the contents of the transactions you are about to purge, then be sure to dump the contents of the Stable Queue Transaction Interface Transaction Cache.

To execute the sysadmin purge_first_open command, log onto the Replication Server and, as the sa account, execute the following command:

```
sysadmin purge_first_open, NumberOfStableQueue,
StableQueueType
```

Purging a single message from a stable queue

You can delete an individual message from a stable queue. To delete an individual message from a stable queue, log onto the Replication Server that manages that particular stable queue and, as the Replication Server sa account, place the Replication Server in stand-alone mode and execute the following command:

```
sysadmin sqm_zap_command, NumberOfStableQueue,
StableQueueType,
IdentityOfSegment, IdentityOfBlock, IdentityOfRowToDelete
go
```

The sysadmin sqm_zap_command command merely marks the message in such a manner as to cause the Replication Server to ignore the marked message.

You can also undelete a deleted message. With the Replication Server still in stand-alone mode, as the Replication Server sa account, execute the following command:

```
sysadmin sqm_unzap_command, NumberOfStableQueue, StableQueueType,
    IdentityOfSegment, IdentityOfBlock, IdentityOfRowToDelete
go
```

The sysadmin sqm_unzap_command command merely removes the delete mark from the message. However, if you restart the Replication Server in normal mode, you will most likely be unable to undelete the row because the message would have been processed by the Stable Queue Manager thread.

Dumping the Data Server Interface outbound stable queue

You can dump and examine the first transaction on a Data Server Interface thread outbound stable queue. To dump the first transaction to the Replication Server's exceptions log, log onto the Replication Server and, as the Replication Server sa, execute the following command:

```
sysadmin log_first_tran, NameOfSQLServer, NameOfDatabase
go
```

The Replication Server exceptions log is a collection of tables (rs_exceptshdr, rs_exceptscmd, and rs_systext) within the Replication Server System Database. This command does not delete the first transaction from the Data Server Interface thread outbound stable queue.

Rebuilding a stable queue

When a Replication Server boots up, it examines its partitions to determine if one is missing or if one has failed. The Replication Server also continues to examine its partitions while it is running. If a Replication Server detects a failed or missing partition, it shuts down the stable queue that is using the failed or missing partition, and logs appropriate error messages about the failure event.

In order to recover from such partition failure events, a Replication Server must:

1. Drop the damaged partitions.
2. Rebuild all stable queues on the partition that failed or is missing. It is not possible to rebuild specific queues at the recovering Replication Server. This is an all-or-nothing proposition.

To recover from a partition failure event, log onto the Replication Server and, as the Replication Server sa account, execute the following command sequence:

```
drop partition LogicalNameOfPartition
go
rebuild queues
go
```

The rebuild queues command is not a means to repair, reclaim, or reconstruct the contents of a particular stable queue. Instead, it is a means to initialize the stable queue. Using the rebuild queues command deletes messages from the replication system, and may make it more difficult to correct other problems in the replication system (e.g., transaction integrity).

The rebuild queues command disconnects all Log Transfer Manager connections to and all Replication Server from the Replication Server where it is executed. Connection attempts (of both types) are refused until the queues are rebuilt. If the Replication Server whose stable queues are being rebuilt is participating in a subscription materialization, be certain to drop the subscription and recreate it, because some data may have been lost from the materialization queue.

If you are rebuilding queues at a Replication Server that controls a source SQL Server, and you suspect that not all required messages are in the source database's transaction log, you should place the Replication Server into stand-alone mode prior to executing the rebuild queues command. Placing the controlling Replication Server in stand-alone mode will ensure that corresponding Log Transfer Managers do not reconnect to the controlling Replication Server before you have completed recovery from old transaction logs.

If you start the Replication Server in stand-alone mode and then execute the rebuild queues command, the Replication Server automatically goes into recovery mode. The Replication Server will only accept connections from Log Transfer Managers that were themselves (subsequently) started in recovery mode. This ensures that the contents of old transaction logs can be resent before current transactions are sent.

Once the stable queues have been rebuilt, the Replication Server can be restarted so that transaction recovery can begin.

Recovering lost transactions

When you execute the rebuild queues command, all immediately downstream Replication Servers perform loss detection for all source SQL Server databases routed to themselves. When the downstream Replication Server performs loss detection, it logs status (and results) messages into its own Replication Server local error log. The downstream Replication Server reports whether it detects a loss. This reporting is at the database level of granularity, not at the transaction ID level of granularity.

Be sure to look for error messages in the log file of the recovering Replication Server. Also, look in the log files of the Replication Server that have direct routes from the recovering Replication Server. If the Replication Server determines that messages were lost, you have to address this problem manually.

The chances of recovering lost messages from any source SQL Server database decreases over time. Stable Queue Managers at destination Replication Servers will be automatically deleting messages on their inbound stable queues (in accordance with the destination site's established save interval). In addition, the source SQL Server database's transaction log may have been truncated.

When a stable queue must be rebuilt at the recovering Replication Server, the recovering Replication Server automatically attempts to recover lost messages. In the process the recovering Replication Server determines if any messages were unable to be recovered from:

1 Stable queue at sites that have a direct route to the recovering Replication Server.
2 The transaction logs of the source databases that the recovering Replication Server is controlling.

Automatic loss detection is conducted at sites immediately downstream from the controlling Replication Server that is being recovered from a partition failure event.

A Replication Server is capable of detecting two types of transaction losses:

1 Stable Queue Manager loss—Refers to the loss of transactions between two Replication Servers.
2 Data Server Interface loss—Refers to the loss of transactions between a controlling Replication Server and a destination SQL Server.

Stable Queue Manager loss is detected by the downstream Replication Server by looking for duplicate messages. If the downstream Replication Server receives a message that it had received before the rebuild queues command was executed (at the Replication Server being recovered), then no messages were lost. However, if the downstream Replication Server receives a message after the rebuild queues command was executed, then one of the following is true:

- Messages were lost between the two Replication Servers
- There were no messages in the downstream's inbound stable queue

In the second case, no messages were lost, but the downstream Replication Server cannot determine this because it has no duplicate messages in the downstream Replication Server's inbound stable queue to verify the fact. This is a false detection of Stable Queue Manager loss. This false detection of Stable Queue Manager loss can be prevented by creating a "heartbeat" between the two Replication Servers, a heartbeat whose interval is less than the downstream Replication Server's save interval. Doing so guarantees that there will always be at least one message in the downstream Replication Server's inbound stable queue that supports the route between the two Replication Servers.

If the downstream Replication Server detects a loss, then no further messages are accepted on the route, and all subsequent messages on that route are rejected.

When a downstream Replication Server does not accept messages, the upstream source is automatically prevented from truncating its stable queue. As a result, the upstream source might run out of stable queue space while the downstream Replication Server handles the Stable Queue Manager loss.

Given the detection of a Stable Queue Manager loss, the first thing one must do is make the decision to recover, or not to recover, from the loss. Either way, one must, as the sa user, log onto that particular Replication Server and execute the command:

```
ignore loss
from NameOfSQLServer.NameOfDatabase
[to {NameOfSQLServer.NameOfDatabase | NameOfReplicationServer}]
go
```

After the Checking Loss message is reported, i.e., before a Stable Queue Manager loss is detected, one can, as the sa, execute the ig nore loss command and thereby disable Stable Queue Manager loss detection for a given source and destination Replication Server pair.

The ignore loss command will force the downstream Replication Server to begin to accept messages again on the route for which the Stable Queue Manager loss was detected. Even after executing the ig nore loss command, a few more messages may be rejected before the downstream Replication Server begins to accept messages over that route. A few more updates to the source database may be necessary before messages begin to flow over that route once again.

If the decision is to continue even though Stable Queue Manager loss has occurred, then nothing further needs to be done as regards Stable Queue Manager loss. However, if the decision is to recover the Stable Queue Manager loss, then one may proceed in either of two ways:

1 Recreate all subscriptions that depend on the affected route.
2 Replay transactions from off-line transaction logs against the source SQL Server(s) controlled by the recovering Replication Server.

The Data Server Interface threads perform loss detection in a way that is similar to the Stable Queue Manager thread loss detection. When retained messages begin arriving from the upstream site(s), the Data Server Interface thread detects a loss depending on whether or not the first message from the origin has already been seen by the Data Server Interface.

If the Data Server Interface detects a loss for a given origin, the Data Server Interface stops accepting and applying all messages to the target database until the ignore loss command is executed for the destination SQL Server database of the Replication Server where the Data Server Interface thread loss was detected.

When is a Replication Server System Database a down Replication Server System Database?

The Replication Server System Database contains a number of tables that support the relationship between a Replication Server and its stable queues:

1 The rs_queues table stores information used by the Replication Server Stable Queue Manager threads to allow site recovery.
2 The rs_queuetext table stores the command, or text, portion of messages on a stable queue.
3 The rs_queuemsg table stores dumps of a stable queue in response to debug commands.

If a partition failure event hits a stable queue that has a relationship to the Replication Server System Database, then the Replication

Server System Database will be subjected to a data integrity corruption event. Furthermore, when these stable queues are rebuilt, the messages in these queues may be lost.

When a Replication Server System Database is subjected to a data integrity corruption event, it will go down. A Replication Server System Database is down when its corresponding Replication Server, or Log Transfer Manager, is unable to access the corrupted Replication Server System Database. It is important to keep in mind that when the Replication Server System Database is down due to a significant corruption event, the corresponding Replication Server cannot be quiesced.

Replication Server System Database corruption

There are many levels of Replication Server System Database corruption severity, ranging from a minor invalid edit of the Replication Server configuration file config.rs, up through those that require the complete reconstruction of the replication system itself.

For any given Replication Server System Database corruption event, there are many possible corruption ripple effects. The number of possible operational Replication Server System Database corruption permutations are not to be taken lightly. The paths that the initial corruption event traverses are specific to the process state of the given Replication Server System Database, and the process states of the replication system as a whole.

You must always keep in mind that a Replication Server System Database is an inherently complex system component. A Replication Server System Database can contain information about:

1. The atomic details of the configuration of the replication system itself.
2. The replicated SQL Server database objects.
3. The physical databases that have been assimilated into the replication system.
4. Any transactions that have failed at a destination SQL Server.
5. The Replication Server objects.
6. The states of the stable queues and messages in the stable queues.
7. The recoverable actions that must be performed at a Replication Server.
8. Replication Server accounts and their permissions.

The following Replication Server System Database data is distributed from the source site (of a route) to destination Replication Servers:

1 Route information.
2 Replication definitions.
3 Replication Server functions.
4 Replication Server error classes.
5 Information about the SQL Server databases that are managed at a source site.

Because the stability of an operating Replication Server system is tightly coupled to the integrity of the data contained within the Replication Server System Database, the corruption of any Replication Server System Database is always a significant threat to the continuing operational viability of a replication system.

Given the complex nature of the interdependencies between tables within a given Replication Server System Database, and between Replication Server System Databases throughout the system, troubleshooting and recovering from a Replication Server System Database data integrity corruption event is extremely complex and not always possible. Due to the critical importance of Replication Server System Database data integrity, it is very important to guard against any and all threats to Replication Server System Database data integrity. Unfortunately, a frequent source of Replication Server System Database corruption is human error; this type of corruption event is not entirely preventable.

One of the most pragmatic ways to manage the risk exposure from user initiated corruption events is to minimize the number of people who have permission to access the Replication Server System Database.

The Replication Server System Database is managed by the SQL Server just like any other physical database. Accordingly, it is best to put the Replication Server System Database transaction log on a device that is separate from the Replication Server System Database itself. Doing so will contribute to avoiding page allocation problems in the SQL Server when the Replication Server System Database transaction log becomes full. In addtion, it enhances your ability to recover the Replication Server System Database when media failure events occur.

Things that sometimes go wrong when you create replication definitions

While a replication definition seems like a simple enough construct to create, things can sometimes go wrong. Here's a list of some of the main things that have been known to cause a replication definition creation cycle to go astray:

1 The controlling Replication Server cannot write the replication definition to its Replication Server System Database. This problem can arise for several reasons:

1.1 You attempt to write to the controlling Replication Server's Replication Server System Database using the wrong SYBASE account login or password. Passwords have a habit of getting changed when you least expect them to.

1.2 The SQL Server that manages the controlling Replication Server's Replication Server System Database has crashed, or has been shut down in a controlled manner.

1.3 The controlling Replication Server's Replication Server System Database does not exist.

2 A destination Replication Server cannot write the replication definition to its Replication Server System Database. This problem can arise for several reasons:

2.1 You attempt to write to the destination Replication Server's Replication Server System Database using the wrong SYBASE account login or password.

2.2 The SQL Server that manages the destination Replication Server's Replication Server System Database has crashed, or has been shut down in a controlled manner.

2.3 The destination Replication Server's Replication Server System Database does not exist.

3 The controlling Replication Server cannot distribute the replication definition to destination Replication Servers. This problem can arise for several reasons:

3.1 You attempt to connect to the destination Replication Server using the wrong SYBASE account login or password.

3.2 The destination Replication Server's Replication Server has crashed, or has been shut down in a controlled manner.

   - **3.3** The route between the controlling Replication Server and the destination Replication Server does not exist.
   - **3.4** The network that connects the controlling Replication Server to the destination Replication Server has crashed, or has been shut down in a controlled manner.

4 The Log Transfer Manager of the controlling Replication Server's Replication Server System Database is not forwarding the replication definition to the controlling Replication Server. This problem can arise for several reasons:

   - **4.1** The Log Transfer Manager of the controlling Replication Server's Replication Server System Database has crashed, or has been shut down in a controlled manner.
   - **4.2** The Log Transfer Manager attempts to connect to the controlling Replication Server using the wrong SYBASE account login or password.
   - **4.3** The Log Transfer Manager cannot make a connection to the controlling Replication Server.

Replication Server recovery

The proper recovery procedure is specific to the failure condition(s) and the manner in which the replication system has been deployed. Attempting to use an inappropriate recovery procedure may complicate the failure condition(s) and require more drastic recovery actions.

Be certain to write down all recovery steps as you perform them, as this will make it easier for SYBASE to provide you with the technical support you may need.

12

Managing changes to a deployed replication system

All of the various things that make up a replication system, such as the SQL Server databases, the function strings, the Data Server Interface threads, or the Log Transfer Managers, arise in a mutually interdependent manner. None of the components of an operating replication system exist as independent entities. The only way a replication system works correctly is when all of its components come together correctly. And, just like every computing system, in order to keep it working correctly, you will have to put in overtime to make changes to your replication system. However, successfully managing changes to a deployed replication system is like walking on rice paper without leaving a trace; much easier said than done.

Your success at managing these changes to your replication system will depend on two main factors:

1 The tools and policies you adopt internally to manage system changes.

2 The procedures you follow to implement changes.

I will not explore the first factor; instead I will present procedures to follow when implementing changes to your replication system. Furthermore, I will limit myself to addressing only those matters of concern that arise from changing or dropping existing components. The creation of all types of replication system components has been previously addressed.

Quiescing the Replication Server

For the majority of the change procedures that will be presented, it is required that you quiesce the replication system (to some degree). Quiescing a Replication Server is done, under normal conditions, to halt traffic between Replication Servers along a given data path, thereby allowing for maintenance on:

- routes
- connections
- replication definitions
- subscriptions
- user-defined functions
- function strings
- function string classes
- stored procedures
- database tables and views
- configuration parameters

The entire replication system will need quiescing if all sites rely on the object undergoing the maintenance activity. If a given Replication Server relies on the object to be changed, then that Replication Server must be quiesced.

If such maintenance activities were to occur when the Replication Server is not quiesced, then:

1. Out-of-sync transactions would arise.
2. Orphaned data rows would arise.
3. Transactions would disappear.
4. The Replication Server System Databases could be severely corrupted.

It is important to keep in mind that when a Replication Server System Database is down due to a significant corruption event, the Replication Server cannot be quiesced.

To quiesce your replication system, do the following:

1. Ensure that all Log Transfer Managers are incapable of continuing to forward transactions to the Replication Server that you are changing. To accomplish this, connect to the SQL Server that manages the source database's Log Transfer Manager and, as the sa, execute the command:

   ```
   suspend log transfer from all
   go
   ```

   Executing the suspend log transfer from all commands will disconnect all corresponding Log Transfer Managers from their source database site's Replication Server. At this point in the process, the corresponding Log Transfer Managers are incapable of forwarding transactions to the Replication Server. You have now prevented all corresponding Log Transfer Managers from reconnecting to that Replication Server, but you have not shut down the corresponding Log Transfer Managers. In addition, you have not stopped messages from arriving at this Replication Server from any other Replication Server that has a route to this particular Replication Server. Furthermore, you have not stopped this particular Replication Server from sending messages to any other Replication Server to which it has a route.

2 Once the suspend log transfer command completes successfully, execute the command:

```
admin quiesce_force_rsi
go
```

The admin quiesce_force_rsi command determines whether the Replication Server is quiescent and forces it to deliver outbound messages. It then waits until acknowledgment has been received. Make sure that remote Replication Server with routes to this Replication Servers are either quiesced, or have their routes suspended during the maintenance activity. A Replication Server is quiescent when all of the following conditions are true:

2.1 Subscription materialization stable queues do not exist.

2.2 A given Replication Server has read all messages in all stable queues.

2.3 No inbound stable queues contain undelivered committed transactions.

2.4 All messages in Replication Server Interface thread outbound stable queues have been sent out to their destinations, and an acknowledgment has been received.

2.5 All messages in Data Server Interface thread outbound stable queues have been applied, and an acknowledgment has been received.

3 Determine if the Replication Server has been quiesced by executing the command:

```
admin quiesce_check
go
```

An error is generated if any of the preceding conditions are not true. Do not proceed until the returned message indicates that the Replication Server is quiesced. If the admin quiesce_check command returned "quiesced," then one can undertake the maintenance activities. However, if the admin quiesce_check command returns "not quiesced," then return to Step 2.

After completing the maintenance activities, you can allow the Log Transfer Managers to reconnect by executing the command:

```
resume log transfer all
go
```

This merely allows the Log Transfer Managers to connect once again, to this Replication Server, but it does not restart any Log Transfer Manager that might have been shut down or crashed. In addition, if routes to this Replication Server have been suspended during the maintenance activity, then reinstate them.

Altering schema components

Any time you alter a physical database object that has been marked for replication, you must proceed with caution. This is especially true when the object is already being processed by the replication system.

Be certain to stop all database operations that will modify the source database object you intend to alter. Do not leave any pending transactions.

When altering schema components, you should follow these general rules:

1. Quiesce the replication system.
2. Alter the source tables and replicate tables, if necessary.
3. Alter the replication definition. To drop columns either from column lists or searchable columns, drop the replication definition and recreate it.
4. Alter existing function strings so they will accept NULLs for the new columns. Function strings associated with a replication definition are not automatically altered when columns are added to a replication definition.
5. Verify that new function strings arrive at replicate Replication Servers.
6. Resume log transfers.

Keep in mind that most of the above commands are asynchronous, so you will have to wait until some transactions have finished.

Dropping schema components

If certain precautions are observed, dropping schema components is a relatively straightforward activity.

When dropping schema components, observe these general rules:

1 Any subscriptions to the replication definition must be dropped first.

2 Confirm that the subscriptions have been dropped at both the replicate as well as the source site. You may want to drop the replicate table, if necessary.

3 Mark the source table as nonreplicated by executing the sp_setreplicate system procedure (setting it to false). You may want to suspend the source database's Log Transfer Manager.

4 Drop the replication definition. This will drop all functions and function strings on all replication servers in the same replication domain.

5 Verify that the replication definition has been dropped at all replication servers.

6 Resume log transfers.

Keep in mind that most of the above commands are asynchronous, so you will have to wait until some transactions have finished.

Determining which databases are under the control of a given Replication Server

Log on to the Replication Server prior to entering any replication definition command. A site at which replication definitions or replicate stored procedures are extant is a source Replication Server. Before proceeding, be absolutely certain that the database has already been placed under the control of the replication system.

You can determine which databases are under the control of a given Replication Server by entering the following query into that Replication Server's Replication Server System Database:

```
select dsname, dbname
from rs_sites, rs_databases
where id = prsid
and name = 'NameOfReplicationServer'
go
```

Dropping a source database from the replication system

If it is required to drop a source database, then it is mandatory that the source database itself be completely inactive, that transactions originating from it have completed their migration through the replication system, and, after attaining these state transitions, that all related database objects and replication objects must be systematically backed out of the replication system before dropping the database itself. In addition, it may be appropriate to drop all of its replicant databases.

If the source SQL Server sa account or database owner drops a Replication Server-controlled source database while the Replication Server is online, then the following Replication Server System Database tables are corrupted: rs_idnames, rs_ids, rs_maintusers, rs_repdbs, rs_repobjs, rs_subscriptions and rs_users. This type of corruption event will cause the replication system to become inoperable. To ensure that this type of Replication Server System Database corruption does not happen, steps must be taken to quiesce the replication system components that interact with the source database, as well as those that interact with any related replicant database(s), before the database is dropped.

Given the replication system is appropriately quiesced, log on to the Replication Server at the destination site and, for each subscription, execute the command

```
drop subscription NameOfSubscription
for NameOfReplicationDefinition
with replicate at NameOfSQLServer.NameOfDatabase without purge
[with suspension]
go
```

The without purge option instructs the Replication Server to leave the rows that were replicated by the subscription in the replicated copy. The with suspension argument suspends the Data Server Interface after the subscription is successfully dropped. You must manually delete the rows for the subscriptions. If you are deleting multiple subscriptions from the same site, then do not use this argument until you are dropping the very last subscription.

Dropping a subscription removes subscription information from the Replication Server System Databases at both the source and destination sites. Check the progress of each drop subscription command at both the source database and destination database sites by executing the following command:

```
check subscription NameOfSubscription
for NameOfReplicationDefinition
with replicate at NameOfSQLServer.NameOfDatabase
go
```

When the subscription becomes invalid at both the source and destination sites, the drop subscription command has completed successfully.

Next, analyze the Data Server Interface thread dedicated to the destination database(s) that are fed by the source database that is to be dropped. For each destination database that is fed by the source database, execute the following command:

```
admin who, dsi
go
```

Find the Data Server Interface for the data server in question. Do not proceed if the state of the Data Server Interface thread is "active." Once all replication subscriptions have been successfully dropped, log onto the Replication Server that controls the SQL Server database you intend to drop, and execute the following command:

```
drop replication definition NameOfReplicationDefinition
go
```

Dropping a replication definition drops any functions and all function strings associated with it. Be aware that dropping a function string can lead to a state where the function string is missing. A missing function string can cause the Data Server Interface to shut down. Analyze the Data Server Interface by executing the following command at the destination Replication Server:

```
admin who, dsi
go
```

You should not be able to find the Data Server Interface for the destination SQL Server database.

After all associated subscriptions have been dropped, connect to the Replication Server that controls the source SQL Server database. As the sa account, remove the source SQL Server database from the replication system by executing the following command:

```
drop connection to NameOfSQLServer.NameOfDatabase
go
```

The drop connection command removes information about the source SQL Server database from the Replication Server System Database. It does not remove any data from the source SQL Server database. However, if the drop connection command fails, then execute the command:

```
sysadmin dropdb, NameOfSQLServer.NameOfDatabase
go
```

The sysadmin dropdb command will force the ID Server to delete the appropriate rows from the rs_idnames table.

After ensuring that the source database is not in use, you can now proceed to drop the source database from the SQL server, if you so choose.

Dropping a replicate database from the replication system

If it is required to drop a replicate database then it is mandatory that:

1. The replicate database itself be completely inactive.
2. Transactions originating from any, and all, source databases have completed their migration through the replication system.
3. All related database objects and replication objects must be systematically backed out of the replication system.

Once all three of these things have completed, you can proceed with dropping the replicate database. It is assumed here that this replicant database does not itself have any replication definitions for its tables or stored procedures. If the replicate database is in fact a mixed database, then you must first complete the tasks for dropping a source database, then continue up through actually dropping the database itself.

If the managing SQL Server sa account drops a replicant database while the Replication Server is online, then the following Replication Server System Database tables are corrupted: rs_idnames, rs_ids, rs_maintusers, rs_repdbs, rs_repobjs, rs_subscriptions and rs_users. This type of corruption event will cause the replication system to become inoperable.

To drop a replicate SQL Server database from the replication system, connect to the Replication Server that controls the replicate site and, for each subscription, execute the command

```
drop subscription NameOfSubscription
for NameOfReplicationDefinition
with replicate at NameOfDataServer.NameOfDatabase without purge
[with suspension]
go
```

The without purge option instructs the Replication Server to leave the rows that were replicated by the subscription in the replicated copy. The with suspension argument suspends the Data Server Interface after the subscription is successfully dropped. You must manually delete the rows for the subscriptions. If you are deleting multiple subscriptions from the same site, then do not use this argument until you are dropping the very last subscription. Dropping a subscription removes subscription information from the Replication Server System Databases at both the source and replicate sites. Check the progress of each drop subscription command by executing, at both the source database and replicant database sites, the following command:

```
check subscription NameOfSubscription
for NameOfReplicationDefinition
with replicate at NameOfSQLServer.NameOfDatabase
go
```

When the subscription becomes invalid at both the source and replicant sites, the drop subscription command has completed successfully. Analyze the Data Server Interface thread dedicated to the replicant database (that is to be dropped) in order to determine its current state.

```
admin who, dsi
go
```

Find the Data Server Interface for the data server in question. Under normal conditions, there is one Data Server Interface thread for each replicant database. Do not proceed if the state of the Data Server Interface thread is "active."

Next, after all subscriptions have been dropped, connect to the Replication Server that manages the replicant database as the sa account, then remove the replicant database from the replication system by executing the command

```
drop connection to NameOfSQLServer.NameOfDatabase
go
```

Executing the above command removes information from the Replication Server System Database. It does not remove any data from the replicant database. However, if the drop connection command fails, then execute the command

```
sysadmin dropdb NameOfSQLServer.NameOfDatabase
```

in order to force the ID Server to delete the rows from the rs_idnames table.

Analyze the Data Server Interface (dedicated to the replicant database that is to be dropped) in order to determine its current state.

```
admin who, dsi
go
```

You should not be able to find the Data Server Interface for the data server. If the Replication Server that manages the replicant database that is to be dropped is not an intermediate site, then execute, at the source Replication Server, the command

```
drop route to NameOfReplicationServer
go
```

If you dropped the route using the nowait clause, then execute the sysadmin purge_route_at_replicate command, at the former destination Replication Server, to remove subscriptions and route information from the system tables at the former destination.

After ensuring that the replicant database is not in use, you can now proceed to drop the replicant database from the SQL server. If a replicant database is not correctly removed from the replication system, then during recovery situations, the connection from the SQL Server might be refused by the replication system's ID Server because the database and its SQL Server might already be registered in the rs_idnames table of the ID Server.

If this is the only replicant database for a given source database, then it is necessary to:

1. Drop all replication definitions at the source SQL Server database.
2. Disable that source SQL Server database's transaction log truncation point.
3. Shut down the source SQL Server database's Log Transfer Manager.

If the Replication Server that supports the replicate SQL Server database you are dropping does not support other replicate SQL Server databases, or is not an intermediate Replication Server site, then:

1. Shut down the destination Replication Server.
2. At the ID Server, drop the destination Replication Server.

Altering connections

The alter connection command allows you to:

1. Change the connection's function string class.
2. Change the connection's error class.
3. Set the new password to use with the login account for connecting to the SQL Server database.
4. Allow, or disallow, the connection to transfer messages to the Replication Server.

The alter connection command does not create the default data manipulation functions, transaction control directive functions, or replication activity coordination functions. In fact, when you alter a connection by setting the associated function string class parameter to a new function string class, you lose the use of any and all data manipulation, transaction control directive, and/or replication activity coordination functions existing at that connection, e.g., rs_usedb, rs_begin, rs_commit, etc.

Before you execute the alter connection command:

1 Use the suspend connection command.
2 Make sure that all required data manipulation, transaction control directive, or replication activity coordination functions and their function strings exist within the new function string class you intend to associate with the connection.

To execute the alter connection command, log onto the Replication Server that controls the connection, and as the Replication Server sa account, execute the following commands:

```
suspend connection to NameOfSQLServer.NameOfDatabase
go
alter connection to NameOfSQLServer.NameOfDatabase
{ set function string class NameOfFunctionStringClass ¦
set error class NameOfErrorClass ¦
set password Password ¦
set log transfer {on ¦ off} }
```

A word to the wise about active replication definitions

Altering replicated tables or stored procedures on the SQL Server affects data replication and should be done with extreme caution! Make these types of changes only after the Log Transfer Manager has processed all records for the replicated object. At minimum, failing to abide by this practice will produce incorrect or unexpected log scans results, and might induce an SQL Server segmentation fault; i.e., you can crash the SQL Server.

Altering a replication definition

You can change an active replication definition by adding new columns to the columns list or to the searchable column list.

Before you alter a replication definition, be certain to quiesce the replication system! To alter a replication definition, log on to the controlling Replication Server, and as the owner of the replication definition or as the Replication Server's sa account, execute the following command:

```
alter replication definition NameOfReplicationDefinition
{add NameOfColumn SYBASEDatatype [,NameOfColumn SYBASEDatatype] ...
add searchable columns NameOfColumn [,NameOfColumn] ...}
go
```

Be sure to modify any associated function strings that they can now accept null data values for the new columns you have added to the replication definition. Be certain not to resume updates against the source SQL Server database base table until all modifications have completed their distribution throughout the entire replication system.

Dropping a replication definition

You can drop extant replication definitions. Before you drop a replication definition, be certain to:

1 Drop all related subscriptions.
2 Execute the sp_setreplicate "false" command against the base source table.
3 Quiesce the replication system.

To drop a replication definition, log on to the controlling Replication Server, and as the owner of the replication definition or as the Replication Server's sa account, execute the following command:

```
drop replication definition NameOfReplicationDefinition
go
```

Dropping subscriptions

It is not possible to alter an extant subscription. In order to make a change to a subscription, you must drop it and then recreate it.

To drop a replicate SQL Server database from the replication system, connect to the Replication Server that controls the replicate site and, for each subscription, execute the command

```
drop subscription NameOfSubscription
for NameOfReplicationDefinition
with replicate at NameOfDataServer.NameOfDatabase without purge
[with suspension]
go
```

The without purge option instructs the Replication Server to leave the rows that were replicated by the subscription in the replicated copy. The with suspension argument suspends the Data Server Interface after the subscription is successfully dropped. You must manually delete the rows for the subscriptions. If you are deleting multiple subscriptions from the same site, do not use this argument until you are dropping the very last subscription. Dropping a subscription removes subscription information from the Replication Server System Databases at both the source and replicate sites. Check the progress of each drop subscription command by executing, at both the source database and replicant database sites, the following command:

```
check subscription NameOfSubscription
for NameOfReplicationDefinition
with replicate at NameOfSQLServer.NameOfDatabase
go
```

When the subscription becomes invalid at both the source and replicant sites, the drop subscription command has completed successfully.

Altering a function

You can change an active function by adding new parameters to the parameters list. Before you alter a function, be certain to quiesce the replication system! To alter a function, log on to the Replication Server where the corresponding replication definition was created and, as the owner of the function or as the Replication Server's sa account, execute the following command:

```
alter function NameOfReplicationDefinition.NameOfFunction
{add parameter @NameOfParameter SYBASEDatatype
[,@NameOfParameter SYBASEDatatype] ...
go
```

Once you alter a function, you might also have to alter its function strings and replicate stored procedures.

Dropping a user-defined function

You can drop an active function. Before you drop a function, be certain to quiesce the replication system! To drop a function, log on to the Replication Server where the corresponding replication definition was created and, as the owner of the function or as the Replication Server's sa account, execute the following command:

```
drop function [NameOfReplicationDefinition.]NameOfFunction
go
```

Dropping a function drops all the function strings for that function from all function string classes. Bear in mind that you cannot drop replication system functions; you can only drop user-defined functions.

Altering a function string

Existing function strings can be altered or restored. Existing function strings must be dropped before new function strings with the same name can be created. Use the alter function string command if both the function and the replication definition are staying. The alter func tion string command executes a drop function string command and a create function string command as a single transaction within the Replication Server System Database.

Before you alter a function string, be certain to quiesce the replication system! To alter a function string, log on to the Replication Server where the corresponding replication definition was created, and as the owner of the function string or as the Replication Server's sa account, execute the following command:

```
alter function string
[NameOfReplicationDefinition.]NameOfFunction[;NameOfFunctionString]
for NameOfFunctionStringClass
[scan 'InputTemplateCharacterString'
[output {language 'OutputTemplateCharacterString'¦
rpc 'execute NameOfTransactSQLStoredProcedure
[@NameOfParameter =] {constant ¦ ?variable!mod?}
[@NameOfParameter =] {constant ¦ ?variable!mod?}] ...'}]
go
```

Changing a function string with function string class scope affects all transactions using the function string class. Altering a function string might affect all subscriptions on all replication definitions within the function string class. When function strings are dropped, any transaction that needs them will fail, causing the Data Server Interface thread within the Replication Server to go down.

Dropping a function string

Existing function strings can be dropped. Before you drop a function string, be certain to quiesce the replication system! To drop a function string, log on to the Replication Server where the corresponding replication definition was created, and as the owner of the function string or as the Replication Server's sa account, execute the following command:

```
drop function string
[NameOfReplicationDefinition.]NameOfFunction[;NameOfFunctionString ¦ all]
for NameOfFunctionStringClass
go
```

Dropping a function string with function string class scope affects all transactions using the function string class. Dropping a function string might affect all subscriptions on all replication definitions within the function string class. When function strings are dropped, any transaction that needs them will fail, causing the Data Server Interface thread within the Replication Server to go down.

Creating function string classes

When you custom-build function string classes, you must ensure that the name of that function string class is globally unique. The Replication Server does not detect function string class name conflicts.

Always create the function string class at a Replication Server that controls a source SQL Server database for which the relevant replication definition(s) have been produced. To create a function string class requires sa permission and the following steps:

1. Create the new globally unique function class.
2. Create all function strings for that class.
3. Suspend the connection to the replicant database.
4. Alter the database connection so that it uses the new function class.
5. Resume the connection to the replicant database.

The default data manipulation functions are only added to the default rs_sql_server_function_class function string class. They are not added by the replication system to any function string class that you create.

The default transaction control directive functions are only added to the default rs_sql_server_function_class function string class. They are not added to any other function string class that you create.

In that all function string classes require data manipulation and transaction control directive functions, you must add them to all custom-made function string classes yourself, as needed. You will always have to add the rs_insert, rs_update, rs_delete, rs_select, and rs_select_with_lock to all custom-made function string classes.

13

The Replication Server Manager

The Replication Server Manager is an application that monitors SQL Servers, Replication Servers, and Log Transfer Managers within a replication system.

To accomplish this, the Replication Server Manager uses Replication Server Manager Agents for a variety of monitoring activity. The function of an agent is to retrieve Replication Server and Log Transfer Manager errors for use by the Replication Server Manager. The agents themselves are a type of object that can, in turn, be monitored by the Replication Server Manager.

The Replication Server Manager executes in one of two modes:

1 Desktop mode—A Motif-based Graphical User Interface application.

2 Command line mode—A command line interface that is run from a UNIX shell or TTY terminal on a local or remote system.

The desktop menu mode

The desktop mode provides a Motif-based Graphical User Interface application that displays the desktop menu. The desktop menu contains five pull-down command menus:

1 System
2 Monitor
3 Configuration
4 Operations
5 Diagnostics

The desktop system menu

The desktop system pull-down menu contains the following commands:

1. Set Up Heartbeat—A heartbeat is an artificial periodic replicated update. The purpose of the heartbeat is to test the connections between a source Replication Server and a destination Replication Server to ensure that they are working properly, and to facilitate the measurement of transaction latency (i.e., the time it takes to distribute a transaction from a source SQL Server database to a destination SQL Server database).
2. Create User Defined View—A user-defined view is a grouping of replication system icons under a single icon. The purpose of the user-defined view is to organize and simplify the desktop.
3. RSM Options—The purpose of this menu item is to enable you to change the behavior of the Replication Server Manager. With this menu item you can specify ping interval, time out, icon status colors, font, and background color. A ping is the means by which the Replication Server Manager periodically determines if a given SQL Server, Replication Server or Log Transfer Manager in the replication system is up and running. You can use the RSM Options Configuration window to specify the ping interval. After the Replication Server Manager pings an SQL Server, Replication Server, or Log Transfer Manager, it waits for an interval to decide whether or not the target is up and running. This interval of time is referred to as the *time out.* You can use the RSM Options Configuration Window to specify the time out. When setting the time out, be certain to take into consideration the physical distances between nodes and the available bandwidth of the network. The RSM Options Configuration Window merely displays the current icon status colors, font, and background color. To change these you must manually edit the underlying configuration files.
4. Event Management—With this command you define asynchronous replication system events and specify the action to take in response to these events. You can define two types of events that trigger an action: Change in Server Status and Partition Utilization Threshold. While you can define different actions for each predefined status, you cannot define different actions for different servers (e.g., all servers that change to a

given status will trigger the same action). You can specify two types of event actions: Desktop Alert and Shell Script/Executable Program. A Desktop Alert is nothing more than a pop-up window running on the Replication Server Manager host computer; it displays a message. A Shell Script or Executable Program can undertake whatever action you custom-build, such as beeping your pager, for example, and relaying a troubleshooting message.

The desktop monitor menu

The desktop monitor pull-down menu contains the following commands:

1. Display Log Files—This command is used to display SQL Server, Replication Server, and Log Transfer Manager error logs. To display the log of a given SQL Server, Replication Server, or Log Transfer Manager, you must select its desktop icon before invoking this pull-down menu item. If you select multiple icons, then all of their error logs are merged, in chronological order, into a single display.
2. Display Heartbeat/Latency—This command is used to display the heartbeat and latency between a given source SQL Server and a given destination SQL Server.

The desktop configuration menu

The desktop configuration pull-down menu contains the following commands:

1. Create Subscription—This command is used to create or define new subscriptions. When you create a subscription, subscription materialization will automatically occur. When you define a subscription you must explicitly initiate the bulk materialization outside of the Replication Server Manager. Before invoking this menu item it is your responsibility to make certain that the appropriate replication definition, route, replicate database, and replicate table exist, that your permissions on the replicate table are appropriate, that the source table has been marked for replication, and that the `sa` login account and password on the source SQL Server database and on each participating Replication Server are the same. When using this menu item, you will have to specify whether you are creating or defining a subscription, select the name of the replication definition from the displayed list of

replication definitions, enter the subscription's predicate expression, select the name of the column to which the predicate expression relates, select the destination SQL Server, and select the materialization method.

2 Examine Catalogs—Use this command to examine the system catalog in order to view the objects contained in a given Replication Server. First you must select a particular Replication Server from the displayed list of Replication Servers. Once you have done that, you can select one of these catalog types: replication definitions, subscriptions, Replication Server user accounts, Replication Server maintenance accounts, or SQL Server databases or routes.

The Replication Definition catalog will present to you the names of the replication definitions, the names of the Replication Servers that control a given source SQL Server database, the names of the source SQL Server databases, the name of the source SQL Server database table, the names of the columns referenced in the replication definition, and some descriptive information. The Subscriptions catalog will present to you the names of the subscriptions, the names of the Replication Servers that control a given destination SQL Server database, the names of the destination SQL Server databases, the names of the corresponding replication definitions. The Replication Users catalog will present to you the names of the Replication Server user accounts, their particular Replication Server, and their password. The Maintenance Users catalog will present to you the names of the Replication Server Maintenance user accounts, their particular Replication Server, their password, and the names of the SQL Server database at which they are used. The Database catalog will present to you the names of the assimilated SQL Server databases, the name of the Replication Server that controls a given SQL Server database, the name of the SQL Server, and its numeric identifier. The Routes catalog will present to you the names of the origin Replication Servers, intermediate Replication Servers and destination Replication Server.

The desktop operations menu

The desktop operations pull-down menu contains the following commands:

1 Connect to Server—This command is used to directly log onto multiple Replication Servers. Before invoking this command, select the icons that represent the Replication Servers that you want to log onto.

2 Shutdown Server—Invoking this menu item is equivalent to issuing the shutdown command. You can use this menu item to shut down a particular Replication Server or Log Transfer Manager. Once you shut down a particular Replication Server or Log Transfer Manager you cannot restart it from within the Replication Server Manager. Before invoking this command, select the icons that represent the Replication Servers or Log Transfer Managers that you want to shut down
3 Quiesce System—This menu item is used to merely flush all queued current messages without shutting down or halting any Replication Servers or Log Transfer Managers within the replication system. The queued messages are merely transmitted between Replication Servers. Nothing is done to stop client processes from continuing to modify source data.

The desktop diagnostics menu

The desktop diagnostics pull-down menu contains the following command options:

1 Verify Route—This command is used to check an individual route between two Replication Servers, or all routes in the replication systems.
2 Verify Subscription—Use this command to determine the current status of a particular subscription.
3 Verify Connection—This command is used to check an individual connection between a given Replication Server and a given SQL Server database, or multiple connections for a given Replication Server, or multiple connections of multiple Replication Servers.
4 Examine Threads—This command is used to examine Replication Server threads of a selected thread type, for a selected Replication Server.
5 Examine Queues—Use this command to examine the stable queues of a selected Replication Server.
6 Partition Utilization—Use this command to graphically represent how much of a selected Replication Server partition is being used.

Command line mode

The command line interface provides a subset of the functions provided by the desktop mode. To use the command line interface you can enter any of the following commands:

1 ?—Lists available Command Line Interface commands.

2 connect *NameOfReplicationServer*—Connects you to the named Replication Server.

3 dbs *list*—Use this command to list the SQL Server databases known to a given Replication Server, or if the optional *list* parameter is omitted, all databases within the replication system.

4 dump_queue—Displays the messages contained on a given stable queue.

5 heartbeat—Forces an artificial replicate update between a source and a destination SQL Server database.

6 info—Use this command to obtain summary information about a given SQL Server, Replication Server or Log Transfer Manager.

7 list—Lists the current sites that the Replication Server Manager is monitoring.

8 mtusers *list*—Use this command to displays information about the authorized replication system Maintenance user logins and their passwords on a given Replication Server, or if the optional list parameter is omitted, all authorized replication system Maintenance user logins and their passwords within the replication system.

9 part—Use this command to obtain summary information about partition usage on a given Replication Server.

10 queues—This command lists the Replication Server's stable queues.

11 quit—Use this command to quit the Replication Server Manager Command Line Interface.

12 repdefs *list*—Use this command to display information about replication definitions on a given Replication Server, or if the optional *list* parameter is omitted, all replication definitions within the replication system.

13 routes *list*—Use this command to display information about routes on a given Replication Server, or if the optional *list* parameter is omitted, all routes within the replication system.

14 shutdown—Shuts down all of the Replication Servers and Log Transfer Managers within the replication system.

15 sites—This command lists the monitored Replication Server sites.

16 status—This command lists the current status of all Replication Servers, SQL Servers, and Log Transfer Managers.

17 subs *list*—Use this command to display information about subscriptions on a given Replication Server, or if the optional *list* parameter is omitted, all subscriptions within the replication system.

18 users *list*—use this command to display information about the authorized replication system user logins and their passwords on a given Replication Server, or if the optional *list* parameter is omitted, all authorized replication system user logins and their passwords within the replication system.

19 verify—Use this command to determine if a given connection or route is working properly.

20 who—A pseudonym for the admin command.

Appendix A

Case studies

High Tech Gadgets Inc. is a fictional international conglomerate that manufactures, sells, and services high-quality gadgets and widgets for business and personal use.

High Tech Gadgets Inc.'s worldwide headquarters is in Toronto, Canada. Corporate-wide manufacturing, marketing, and services are overseen by the Toronto office. Normal day-to-day operations are managed at the local business sites. Because of the high demand for gadgets and replacement widgets, the company's manufacturing, sales, and services sites around the world are open for business seven days a week, twenty-four hours a day, 365 days a year.

High Tech Gadgets uses telemarketing to sell their product. Their phone sales centers are located in Des Moines, Iowa, USA; Brussels, Belgium; and Bangkok, Thailand. Their manufacturing and assembly plants are located in Singapore and in Tijuana, Mexico. To provide their customer with post-sales support, High Tech Gadgets Inc. has service centers in every major city in the first world.

At present, High Tech Gadgets, Inc. uses a distributed autonomous network of SYBASE SQL Servers to store and manage their business information. Each local business site captures and manages locally the data it needs to support its own business processes.

The CIO of High Tech Gadgets has been chartered with the task of improving access to data. The CIO's architects have analyzed the conglomerate's business needs and, based on High Tech Gadgets' business process models, has chosen to develop and deploy four SYBASE Replication Server projects intended to improve worldwide data access.

Case 1 - Distribution of marketing information

High Tech Gadgets telemarkets a wide variety of gadgets. To promote a consistent presentation of High Tech Gadgets products, the marketing group wants to provide telemarketers with product and sales promotion data. The decision has been made to replicate read-only product and sales promotion data (produced by the Toronto-based marketing group) to each telemarketing center. Fortunately, each phone sales center uses the same application and the same physical database model. In addition, the physical structure of the product and sales promotion tables used by the marketing group are identical to their counterparts at the phone sales centers.

While all sites will get the same product information, not all sites will receive the same sales promotion data. The plan calls for data from two tables in the marketing group's database to be replicated; the product table and the sales promotion table.

The replication definition for the product table will look something like this:

```
create replication definition ProductRepDef
with primary at MarketingServer.MarketingServerDatabase
(ProductID int , ...)
primary key (ProductID)
searchable columns (ProductID ...)
```

The replication definition for the sales promotion table will look something like this:

```
create replication definition SalePromotionRepDef
with primary at MarketingServer.MarketingServerDatabase
(SalePromotionID int, DesMoines tinyint, Brussels tinyint, Bangkok tinyint, ...)
primary key (SalePromotionID)
searchable columns (SalePromotionID ...)
```

When the marketing group wants a particular phone sales center to offer a sale promotion, it sets that phone sales site indicator to 1.

A subscription to the product table is created at each phone sales center:

```
create subscription ProductSubscription
for ProductRepDef
with replicate at ...
```

At the Des Moines phone sales center they create the following subscription to the sales promotion table:

```
create subscription ProductSubscription
for SalePromotionRepDef
with replicate at DesMoinesServer.DesMoinesDatabase
where DesMoines = 1
```

At the Brussels phone sales center they create the following subscription to the sales promotion table:

```
create subscription ProductSubscription
for SalePromotionRepDef
with replicate at BrusselsServer.BrusselsDatabase
where Brussels = 1
```

At the Bangkok phone sales center they create the following subscription to the sales promotion table:

```
create subscription ProductSubscription
for SalePromotionRepDef
with replicate at BangkokServer.BangkokDatabase
where Bangkok = 1
```

Case 2 - Consolidation of accounting groups

The first phase of the project, to consolidate accounting back in the Toronto office, requires product and customer sales data to be replicated to the Toronto office from each phone sales center.

The phone sales centers capture product sales data and customer data. The physical database model that the sales system uses contains a customer subject area and a product sales subject area. Each of these subject areas is, in turn, composed of multiple tables. However, not all attributes about product sales and customers being captured by the sales system is of value to the accountants.

Due to the static nature, and narrower scope, of accounting practices, the choice was made to have the Toronto accounting office subscribe to a subset of customer and product sales information from the telemarketing centers. These subscription fragments map directly to the accounting application's physical data model.

The key to providing the system solution involves creation of replication definitions that cover vertical fragments of the source tables, and subscriptions that cover all rows in the source tables.

Case 3 - Wireless Replication System

The service centers are responsible for providing post-sales support. Customers contact their local service center and place orders for on-site service. The existing SQL Server-based customer service system records and assigns the service requests to field service representatives, who arrive at the service center to pick up their work orders at the start of their shift. If the service request orders are re-prioritized during the day, the affected field service representatives are paged, and must return to the service center to pick up their updated work orders.

At the end of each shift the field service representative must log onto the inventory application and enter the quantity and part numbers of widgets consumed during the day's shift. And, following that task, they must log onto the billing system and produce the new service bills for that day's shift.

High Tech Gadgets has decided to participate in the alpha program to test a new SYBASE sessionless transmissions Open Client API, and to test another vendor's wide-area wireless PCMCIA modem. Because the Open Client API uses a sessionless transmission protocol, the connection costs for wireless communications are significantly reduced. The purpose of the alpha program is to prove whether or not it is really cost-effective for High Tech Gadgets Inc. to:

1 Forward service calls to mobile field service representatives during the day.
2 Further automate inventory tracking.
3 Further automate billing for service calls.

A small, low-volume service center has been selected as the pilot site.

Currently, field service representatives are provisioned with their own set of repair tools, a light inventory of replacement widgets, and a vehicle. For the purpose of the alpha program, the vehicles will be upgraded as follows:

1 The vehicle will contain a portable computer, with a bar code scanner and a printer.
2 Each portable computer will run Windows NT, the SYBASE System 10 SQL Server, a new version of the SYBASE Replication Server, and the new field service representative application. The mobile SYBASE Replication Server will use the sessionless transmissions Open Client API.

At the service center, the field service requests, recorded by the service order system, are managed by a System 10 SQL Server. The service order system will be extended to support a SYBASE Replication Server that also uses the sessionless transmissions Open Client API. The SYBASE Replication Server Replication Server Interface thread at the service center will use the sessionless transmissions Open Client API to replicate service request orders to specific field service representatives.

The sessionless transmissions Open Client API can support the ability of a Replication Server Interface thread to place a wireless call to another enhanced SYBASE Replication Server, and automatically disconnect when the outbound messages have been received by a mobile Replication system. The mobile Replication system's Data

Server Interface thread will then apply the message stream to the mobile SQL Server.

The enhanced mobile SYBASE Replication Server will place a wireless call to the stationary service center's Replication Server and automatically disconnect when the outbound messages have been received by the stationary service center's Replication system. The enhanced mobile SYBASE Replication Server will use the sessionless transmissions Open Client API to handle normal transaction messages, as well as asynchronous procedure calls.

During the pilot program, field service representatives will keep their service vehicles at their residences. When a field service representative starts their shift, they will log onto their vehicle's portable computer. This logon event re-establishes the connections from the service center to the mobile Replication Server and from the mobile Replication Server to the service center. With the two connections reestablished, the work orders are transmitted to the vehicle's portable computer, and the field service representatives are ready to begin their work.

In conjunction with the new mobile end user application, the field service representative will use a bar code scanner to record the identity of widgets consumed per work order. These entries will automatically generate a pending service bill. After completing each service call, the field service representative will complete the service bill.

Whenever a wigdet is scanned, a record of that event is recorded in a table in the mobile SQL Server database. The stationary service center's SQL Server subscribes to all mobile SQL Server databases. These inventory depletion events are then replicated from the mobile SQL Server databases to the service center's SQL Server, where the inventory system has ready access. The inventory system is now capable of tracking inventory changes throughout the day.

Whenever a service bill is completed, a record of that event is recorded in a table in the mobile SQL Server database. The completed service bills are then replicated from the mobile SQL Server databases to the service center's SQL Server where the billing system has ready access. The billing system is now capable of processing bills throughout the day.

If there is a mismatch between the issued work order and the actual customer service needs, the field service representative will use the new mobile end user application to change the original work order. These changes will be implemented using the Replication Server's asynchronous procedure call features.

Once a customer service request is finished, the field service representative will query their mobile SQL Server to retrieve their next work order assignment. If work orders have been reassigned or reprioritized during the day, the service center merely replicates the modifications to the appropriate field service representative's mobile SQL Server, where they are detected by the field service representative when they query their mobile SQL Server.

Case 4 - Global funds management

High Tech Gadgets has a division that manages the employee's pension funds, to which it matches each employee's dollar contribution, up to five percent of the employee's annual salary. There are a number of funds in which the employee can elect to place their pension monies. The majority of these pension funds are managed with the intention to protect principal and, so, are low risk, low yield, funds. However, the manager of the funds has decided to create a new high yield, high risk fund that is based on derivative instruments.

To manage this new derivatives based pension fund, the division manager has decided to trade derivative instruments twenty-four hours a day. Derivatives trading will take place out of the Toronto, Brussels and Singapore offices. Over the course of the day, the derivative instruments pension fund's book will be passed from office to office, and ownership of the book will reside in the office that is in possession of the book.

Of the three sites, only the site that owns the book is authorized to modify data. However, when the book is about to be passed, there is an short period of time in which two sites will be authorized to modify data: the primary site that intends to rescind ownership, and the secondary site that intends to assume ownership. During these ownership transition phases, all data modifications originating from the secondary site are pending transactions until the primary site approves the trade or disapproves the trade.

As the SYBASE Replication Server in a loosely coupled system that only supports the direct modification of source data and not replicate data, both the physical data model for the derivatives system and the client processes that will read and modify that data will have to be significantly extended.

As regards to the physical data model, all entities will have to contain the following:

1 Each site will contain its own data, as well as all data from both of the other two sites.

2 Row IDs that are guaranteed to be globally unique.

3 A nonnullable attribute that indicates which site originated each data row. It has been decided that a user-defined SYBASE datatype will represent this attribute. The base datatype of this user-defined SYBASE datatype is the nonnullable char. In addition, to ensure the integrity of the data values that will be used to instantiate this attribute, a SYBASE rule will be bound to this attribute.

4 A nonnullable attribute that indicates which primary site currently owns each data row. It has been decided that a user-defined SYBASE datatype will represent this attribute. The base datatype of this user-defined SYBASE datatype is the nonnullable char. In addition, to ensure the integrity of the data values that will be used to instantiate this attribute, a SYBASE rule will be bound to this attribute.

5 The row ID will be extended to include a numeric sequence attribute.

6 Each row will carry the identity of the SYBASE login account that created or modified it.

7 Each row will carry an originating site timestamp.

8 Each row will carry a local site timestamp.

9 Each table will be extended to include a Boolean indicator for logical deletion.

10 A site lookup table will be contained within each site's database. The site lookup table will contain a string literal that will be instantiated with the identity of the local site.

11 Triggers will be built to prohibit local transactions from modifying data rows whose ownership is nonlocal. The purpose of the trigger will be to compare the originating site's transaction parameter to the identity of the local site (stored within the local lookup table). If these two variables match then the transaction is allowed to commit, else it is rolled back. The trigger will also examine the parameter that indicates the identity of the SYBASE login account that originates the transaction. If the Replication Server maintenance user originates the transaction, then it will be allowed to commit, else it could be rolled back (if it is nonlocal and if it is not a SYBASE login account that is authorized to submit asynchronous procedure calls).

12 The rs_update function strings will have to be implemented as an insert transaction that is able to increment the row ID's sequence number.

13 The rs_update and rs_insert function strings will have to be modified to place the literal data value in the local site timestamp parameter written into the originating site timestamp column.

14 The rs_delete function strings will have to be implemented such that physical deletes do not occur, but, instead, the data row is logically deleted by setting a Boolean indicator for deletion.

15 Triggers will have to be written to prohibit physical deletion of data rows.

As regards to the client processes, they will have to:

1 Be able to determine the single site at which a given data row will have to be directly modified.

2 Each transaction will contain a parameter that indicates the identity of the originating site.

3 Each transaction will contain a parameter that indicates the identity of the SYBASE login account that originates the transaction.

4 Each update transaction will have to be implemented as an insert transaction that is able to increment the row ID's sequence number.

5 Each select transaction will have to be implemented to retrieve the row ID with the maximum sequence number.

6 Each delete transaction will have to be implemented such that physical deletes do not occur, but, instead, the data row is logically deleted by setting a Boolean indicator for deletion.

7 Each select transaction will have to be implemented such that they only select data rows that have not been marked for deletion.

8 Transactions will have to be implemented to support the transference of data row ownership from one primary site to another.

9 In the event that a primary site is unavailable for an unacceptable period of time, then the client processes, at a designated failover site, must be able to submit a corresponding suite of transactions that are capable of modifying nonlocal data. Another literal string value will be

written to the local lookup table so that the failover site can modify the primary site's data, as well as its own data.

10 Each computer that is the host to a client process will provide the client with a stable queue. The queue will contain transactions that have been submitted to the SQL Server, and which can be resubmitted to a failover site in the event that the local SQL Server crashes resulting in lost client transactions. The client transaction stable queue will be automatically managed by the client process, but will support runtime intervention in the case where a crashed local SQL Server has lost transactions which must be subsequently applied at the failover site.

As regards to the system design as a whole, it will have to address:

1 The failure of a SQL Server at a site that owns the book, where the corresponding Log Transfer Manager and controlling Replication Server is not capable of distributing the active transactions. The contents of their queue will have to be flushed, and any lost transaction will have to be manually entered.

2 The failure of a SQL Server, Log Transfer Manager and Replication Server at a site that owns the book. The manual recovery heuristics will use the originating site, owner site, sequence number, originating site timestamp, and local site timestamp attributes to facilitate recovery and regaining of data integrity.

3 The loss of transaction messages due to the failure of a network that supports a Replication Server route. The manual recovery heuristics will use the originating site, owner site, and sequence number, originating site timestamp, and local site timestamp attributes to facilitate recovery and regaining of data integrity.

Appendix B

Queries to assist the Replication Server Administrator

Who owns a particular replication definition?

```
select username
from rs_users, rs_objects
where rs_users.uid = rs_objects.ownend
and rs_objects.objname = NameOfReplicationDefinition
```

What are all of the columns in a replication definition?

```
select colname
from rs_columns, rs_objects
where rs_columns.objid = rs_objects.objid
and rs_objects.objname = NameOfReplicationDefinition
```

Which columns in a replication definition are in the primary key?

```
select colname
from rs_columns, rs_objects   ..
where rs_columns.objid = rs_objects.objid
and rs_objects.objname = NameOfReplicationDefinition
and rs_columns.primary = 1
```

Which columns in a replication definition are searchable?

```
select colname
from rs_columns, rs_objects
where rs_columns.objid = rs_objects.objid
and rs_objects.objname = NameOfReplicationDefinition
and rs_columns.searchable = 1
```

What are the replication definitions in a particular primary database, for a particular data server?

```
select objname
from rs_databases, rs_objects
where rs_databases.dbid = rs_objects.dbid
and rs_databases.dsname = NameOfSQLServer
and rs_databases.dbname = NameOfSQLServerDatabase
```

Which replication server manages a particular replication definition?

```
select name
from rs_sites, rs_objects
where rs_sites.id = rs_objects.prsid
and rs_objects.objname = NameOfReplicationDefinition
```

How much total partition space is available and how much of it is being used?

```
select sum(allocated_segs) "total", sum(num_segs) "used"
from rs_diskpartitions
```

How much space is each inbound LTM queue consuming?

```
select dsname, dbname, sum(used_flag) "#segs"
from rs_segments, rs_databases
where rs_databases.dbid = rs_segments.q_number
and rs_segments.q_type = 1
group by dsname, dbname
```

How much space is each DSI queue consuming?

```
select dsname. dbname, sum(used_flag) "#segs"
from rs_segments, rs_databases
where rs_databases.dbid = rs_segments.q_number
and rs_segments.q_type = 0
group by dsname, dbname
```

How much space are RSI queues consuming?

```
select name, sum(used_flag) "#segs"
from rs_segments, rs_sites
where rs_sites.id = rs_segments.q_number
group by name
```

How much space are materialization/dematerialization queues consuming?

```
select dsname, dbname, subname, sum(used_flag) "#segs"
from rs_segments, rs_databases, rs_subscriptions
where rs_databases.dbid = rs_segments.q_number
```

```
and rs_segments.q_type not in (0, 1 )
and substring(rs_subscriptions.subid, 5, 4) = rs_segments.q_number
group by dsname, dbname, subname
```

NOTE: For (de)materialization queues, q_type is equal to the lower 4 bytes of subid.

What are all the origin queue ids stored in a stable queue?

```
select origin_q_id, valid, dsname, dbname
from rs_databases, rs_oqid
where rs_databases.dbid = rs_oqid.origin_site_id
and rs_oqid.q_number = IDNumberOfQueue
and rs_oqid.q_type = TypeOfQueue
```

NOTE: The rs_oqid table actually logs what is in the stable queue. It is periodically refreshed.

What are the RSI locaters that an RS has received?

```
select name, locater
from rs_sites, rs_locater
where rs_sites.id = rs_locater.sender
and rs_locater.type = 'R'
```

What are the distributor and executor (in-bound LTM queue) locaters?

```
select dsname, dbname, locater, type
from rs_dataqbases, rs_locater
where rs_dataqbases.id = rs_locater.sender
and rs_locater.type in ( 'D', 'E')
```

NOTE: The distributor locater corresponds to the last subscription message.

NOTE: The Executor locater corresponds to the LTM truncation point returned to the LTM.

What are the application supplied transaction names of the transactions dumped?

```
select distinct(tran_name), tran_id, origin_time, origin_user
from rs_queuemsg
group by tran_id
```

NOTE: The same name may be present for multiple transactions. The data value of tran_id is globally unique though.

What are the actual statements in a transaction in the dumped portion of the queue?

```
select rs_queuemsgtxt.txt, rs_queuemsgtxt.seg
from rs_queuemsgtxt, rs_queuemsg
where rs_queuemsg.q_number = rs_queuemsgtxt.q_number
and rs_queuemsg.q_row = rs_queuemsgtxt.q_row
and rs_queuemsg.q_seg = rs_queuemsgtxt.q_seg
and rs_queuemsg.q_blk = rs_queuemsgtxt.q_blk
and rs_queuemsg.q_type = rs_queuemsgtxt.q_type
and rs_queuemsg.tran_id = GloballyUniqueTransactionID
order by rs_queuemsgtxt.q_seg, rs_queuemsgtxt.q_blk, rs_queuemsgtxt.q_row,
rs_queuemsgtxt.q_seg
```

What databases have subscriptions against any replication definitions in a given primary database?

```
select distinct (rs_repdbs.dsname + '.' + rs_repdbs.dbname)
from rs_subscriptions, rs_repdbs, rs_objects, rs_databases
where rs_objects.dbid = rs_databases.dbid
and rs_subscriptions.dbid = rs_repdbs.dbid
and rs_subscriptions.objid = rs_objects.objid
and rs_databases.dbname = 'NameOfSQLServerDatabase'
and rs_databases.dsname = 'NameOfSQLServer'
```

NOTE: This query applies only in a primary site RSSD.

NOTE: The join with rs_repdbs is used to get the replicate database name. The joins with rs_objects and rs_databases restrict the search to just the replication definitions that are in the primary database of interest.

What databases have subscriptions to a given replication definition?

```
select distinct (rs_repdbs.dsname + '.' + rs_repdbs.dbname)
from rs_subscriptions, rs_repdbs, rs_objects
where rs_subscriptions.objid = rs_objects.objid
and rs_subscriptions.dbid = rs_repdbs.dbid
and rs_objects.objname = 'NameOfReplicationDefinition'
```

NOTE: This query applies only in a primary site RSSD.

List the replication definitions that a given replicate database subscribes to.

```
select distinct (objname)
from rs_subscriptions, rs_objects, rs_databases
where rs_subscriptions.dbid = rs_databases.dbid
and rs_subscriptions.objid = rs_objects.objid
```

```
and rs_databases.dsname = 'NameOfSQLServer'
and rs_databases.dbname = 'NameOfSQLServerDatabase'
```

NOTE: This query applies only in a replicate site RSSD.

What is the primary database of a given subscription?

```
select rs_databases.dsname, rs_databases.dbname
from rs_subscriptions, rs_objects, rs_databases
where rs_objects.dbid = rs_databases.dbid
and rs_subscriptions.objid = rs_objects.objid
and rs_subscriptions.subname = 'NameOfReplicationSubscription'
```

NOTE: This works only for application subscriptions. For RSSD subscriptions, use *pdbid* field in rs_subscriptions instead of *dbid.*

What is the controlling primary RS for a given subscription?

```
select rs_sites.name
from rs_subscriptions, rs_objects, rs_sites
where rs_objects.prsid = rs_sites.id
and rs_subscriptions.objid = rs_objects.objid
and rs_subscriptions.subname = 'NameOfReplicationSubscription'
```

NOTE: This query applies only in a replicate site RSSD.

What primary databases does a given database subscribe to, if the given database is not an RSSD?

```
select rs_databases.dsname, rs_databases.dbname
from rs_databases
where rs_databases.dbid in
(select distinct (rs_objects.dbid)
from rs_subscriptions, rs_objects, rs_databases
where rs_subscriptions.dbid = rs_databases.dbid
and rs_subscriptions.objid = rs_objects.objid
and rs_subscriptions.pdbid = 0
and rs_databases.dbname = 'NameOfSQLServerDatabase'
and rs_databases.dsname = 'NameOfSQLServer')
```

NOTE: This query applies only in a replicate site RSSD.

NOTE: rs_subscriptions for application subscriptions does not directly include the primary database. It is obtained by finding the primary db of the replication definition. This makes it easier to move the primary site.

What primary databases does a given database subscribe to, if the given database is an RSSD?

```
select rs_databases.dsname, rs_databases.dbname
from rs_databases
where rs_databases.dbid in
(select distinct (pdbid)
from rs_subscriptions
where pdbid != 0)
```

NOTE: This query applies only in a replicate site RSSD.

NOTE: RSSD subscriptions have the primary database embedded in the rs_subscriptions table.

What are the clauses in a given subscription?

```
select rs_columns.colname, valuetype,
low_flag, low_len, substring (low_value, 1, low_len) "low_value",
high_flag, high _len, substring (high _value, 1, high _len) " high _value",
from rs_subscriptions, rs_rules, rs_columns
where rs_rules.colnum = rs_columns.colnum
and rs_rules.objid = rs_columns.objid
and rs_subscriptions.subid = rs_rules.subid
and rs_subscriptions.subname = 'NameOfReplicationSubscription'
```

What are all the functions associated with a Replication Definition?

```
select rs_functions.funcname
from rs_functions, rs_objects
where rs_functions.objid = rs_objects.objid
and rs_objects.objname = 'NameOfReplicationDefinition'
```

Is the output function string for a given function name, table and dataserver.database automatically generated (default function string), or is there a user specified output template for the function?

```
select rs_funcstrings.attributes & 32, rs_funcstrings.fstringid,
rs_funcstrings.classid, rs_funcstrings.name,
from rs_funcstrings, rs_functions, rs_objects, rs_databases
where rs_databases.dsname = 'NameOfSQLServer'
and rs_databases.dbname = 'NameOfSQLServerDatabase'
and rs_databases.funcclassid = rs_funcstrings.classid
and rs_functions.funcid = rs_funcstrings.funcid
and rs_functions.funcname = 'NameOfFunction'
and rs_objects.objname = 'NameOfReplicationDefinition'
and rs_objects.objid = rs_functions.objid
```

NOTE: If a default function string is used, then the attributes columns in rs_funcstrings will indicate so (query below will return 32). In that case, there will be no function string stored in the RS—it will be automatically generated on the fly.

NOTE: This query may return multiple rows if multiple instances of the function exist.

What is the actual output template given the function string id, and class id?

```
select rs_systext.textval
from rs_systext, rs_ functions
where rs_funcstrings.fstringid = rs_systext.parentid
and rs funcstrings.funcid = function_id
and rs_funcstrings.classid = class_id
and rs_syst.texttype = 'O'
order by rs_systext.sequence
```

What are the class wide function string for a given class?

```
select rs_funcstrings.name, rs_systextval.textval
from rs_systext, rs_funcstrings, rs_functions, rs_classes
where rs_funcstrings.funcid = rs_functions.funcid
and rs_funcstrings.fstringid = rs_systexl.parentid
and rs_funcstrings.classid = rs_classes.classid
and rs_classes.classname = 'NameOfFunctionClass'
and rs_systext.texttype = 'O'
and rs_functions.objid = 0X00
order by rs_funcstrings.funcid, rs_systext.sequence
```

NOTE: Some of the class wide function string may be automatically generated, so not all class wide functions' output templates will be returned by the query.

What are the parameters for a user defined table-scope function?

```
select rs_columns.colname, rs_columns.coltype
from rs_columns, rs_functions
where rs_columns.objid = rs_functions.funcid
and rs_functions.funcname = 'NameOfFunction'
```

Determine which databases are under the control of a given RS
Log onto the RS prior to entering any replication definition command. A site at which replication definitions are extant, is a source RS.

WARNING: Before proceeding, be absolutely certain that the database (containing the tables for which replication definitions are to be created) has been placed under the control of the replication system.

NOTE: You can determine which databases are under the control of a given RS by entering the following query into that RS's RSSD

```
select dsname, dbname
from rs_sites, rs_databases
where id = prsid
and name = 'NameOfReplicationServer'
go
```

Glossary

asynchronous procedure call Produced by executing a replicated stored procedure that has been explicitly coupled to a user-defined function within the Replication system.

atomic materialization The default subscription materialization method for the Replication Server. With atomic materialization a holdlock is always taken on the source data table. To invoke this method do not use either the without holdlock option, or the incrementally option in your create subscription command.

bulk materialization This approach allows you to load source data for a subscription from media rather than pass it through the network from the source to the destination.

connection A message stream from a controlling Replication Server to the controlled SQL Server database.

daemon process A process that executes without a terminal or login shell associated with it. Typically, daemon processes wait until some other process notifies it of an event, upon which it will perform a predefined action.

dAIO Manages asynchronous I/O operations to stable queues for the Replication Server.

dALARM Keeps track of alarms set by other threads.

Data Server Interface thread There is one Data Server Interface thread (and accompanying Stable Queue Transaction Interface thread) for each target SQL Server (or Open Server process) a given Replication Server writes to. A given Replication Server can support multiple Data Server Interface threads. The function of the Data Server Interface thread is to: 1.) Read a given outbound Data Server Interface thread stable queue, via a dedicated Stable Queue Transaction Interface thread; 2.) As the database maintenance user, apply transactions to the SQL Server that manages the target replicate database.

dCM Manages connections to SQL Servers, to other Replication Servers and to Open Server programs.

Distributed Database System A computing system that contains a number of autonomous database management systems (not necessarily all SYBASE SQL Servers) that are interconnected by a network, and that cooperate with each other when performing data access and data capture tasks.

Distributor thread Exists for each database under the control of a given Replication Server. At boot time the Replication Server starts up each of its Distributor threads, and sets up each inbound stable queue that supports a given Distributor thread. The purpose of the Distributor thread is to: 1.) Read transactions from a given inbound stable queue, via a dedicated Stable Queue Transaction Interface thread; 2.) Determine which subscribed transactions a particular data server is interested in; 3.) Forward subscribed transactions onto target data servers.

dSUB Sleeps for a period of time (a configurable quantum), then wakes up to attempt to restart any subscriptions that have failed.

Executor thread A Log Transfer Manager Open Client connection to the Replication Server. A Replication Server can handle multiple concurrent Executor threads. There will be one Executor thread for each Log Transfer Manager-to-Replication Server connection. The Executor has two main tasks: 1.) Verifies that Log Transfer Manager submissions are normalized; 2.) Writes the Log Transfer Manager submissions onto a dedicated stable queue.

function A Replication Server function is the declaration of the name of a database operation, and its associated (optional) parameter list.

function call A Replication Server function call is a request that consists of the name of the function and an initialized list of data parameters.

function string While a Replication Server function merely states what action is intended, the Replication Server function string specifies exactly how the action will be undertaken.

function string class A Replication Server function string class is the name of a set of all function strings used within a particular database.

heartbeat A heartbeat is an artificial periodic replicated update. The purpose of the heartbeat is to test the connections between a source Replication Server and a destination Replication Server to ensure that they are working properly, and to facilitate the measurement of transaction latency.

ID Server A special Replication Server within a Replication Server domain. The function of the ID Server is to register all Replication Servers, and all SQL Server databases within the Replication system.

incremental atomic materialization An approach that is invoked by using the incrementally option of the create subscription command. When the incrementally option is specified, the destination Replication Server applies the source data rows in batch, so that data appears at the replicate a batch at a time. The use of this batch initialization technique avoids long running open transactions; there can be a very serious problem with large source tables. When the incrementally option is used, the select is performed (by the destination Replication Server) with a holdlock so that serial consistency with the source is maintained. The replicate table eventually passes through the states that occurred previously at the source.

latency The time it takes to distribute a transaction from a source SQL Server database to a destination SQL Server database.

Log Transfer Manager An Open Server/Open Client application that monitors an SQL Server's transaction log, and detects changes to a primary SQL Server database and passes those changes onto a Replication Server process.

Message Delivery Module Called by the Distributor thread, it has passed to it the transaction row and the name of the destination Replication Server. Uses in memory routing information (contained in the RSSD.rs_routes table), the Message Delivery Module determines the next site that will receive the transaction row.

nonatomic materialization An approach that is invoked by using the without holdlock option of the create subscription command. This approach differs from the atomic materialization method in that the nonatomic materialization approach uses the rs_select default data manipulation system function, rather than rs_select_with_lock default data manipulation system function to retrieve data from the source database.

ping The means by which the Replication Server Manager periodically determines if a given SQL Server, Replication Server or Log Transfer Manager in the Replication system is up and running.

ping interval The period of time between pings in the Replication system.

replicated stored procedure A Transact-SQL stored procedure that has been marked for replication.

replication definition A formal description of a source SQL Server database table, whose data you want to be replicated to one or more destination SQL Server database tables.

Replication Server The SYBASE Replication Server (RS) is an asynchronous mechanism that supports the continuous replication and distribution of *subscribed* transactions. The Replication Server is a multithreaded Open Server/Open Client application that maintains replicated data at multiple sites on a network and processes data transactions received from other Replication Servers on the network. In addition, the Replication Server distributes replication and subscription information to other Replication Servers.

Replication Server Interface thread Replication Server Interface thread is an asynchronous Open Client connection. A Replication Server uses the RS_RS_user login name and password to establish Open Client connections with another Replication Server. There will be a Replication Server Interface thread for each remote Replication Server that the local Replication Server forwards transactions to. Each Replication Server Interface thread has its own dedicated Stable Queue Manager thread. All transaction rows (in the form of function calls), written by the dedicated Stable Queue Manager on behalf of a Distributor thread, remain in storage on an outbound stable queue until they are successfully sent to the remote Replication Server by the Replication Server Interface thread.

Replication Server Interface USER thread An Open Client connection to the Replication Server. This thread is used to handle messages coming from a remote Replication Server to this Replication Server. The Replication Server Interface USER thread calls the Message Delivery Module to decide where to send a given message. If the message is for an SQL Server that the Replication Server supports then the message is written to a Data Server Interface thread outbound stable queue. If the message is destined for another Replication Server, then it is written to a Replication Server Interface thread outbound stable queue.

Replication Server Manager An application that monitors SQL Servers, Replication Servers, and Log Transfer Managers within a Replication system.

Replication Server Manager Agent Retrieves Replication Server and Log Transfer Manager errors for use by the Replication Server Manager.

Replication Server Manager Command Line Interface A command line interface to the Replication Server Manager application that is run from a UNIX shell or TTY Terminal, on a local or remote system.

Replication Server Manager Desktop A Motif-based Graphical User Interface to the Replication Server Manager application.

Replication Server System Database A special SYBASE database within which is stored Replication Server system information, such as replication definitions, routes, and replication subscriptions. Each and every Replication Server within the Replication system has its own Replication Server System Database.

Replication Server USER thread An Open Client connection to the Replication Server. The sole purpose of this thread is to create or drop replication subscriptions at the primary Replication Server.

route A message stream from a Replication Server to another Replication Server.

stable queue Used by the Replication Server to spool messages.

Stable Queue Manager thread Manages access to, and the organization of, a given stable queue. The Stable Queue Manager is responsible for: 1.) Reclaiming space in outbound stable queues after transactions have been forwarded; 2.) Reclaiming space in inbound stable queues when a transaction has been rolled back.

Stable Queue Transaction Interface thread Any Replication Server thread that reads from a stable queue does so via its own dedicated Stable Queue Transaction Interface thread. The Stable Queue Transaction Interface thread monitors, and orders, transactions that reach the Replication Server. Like Stable Queue Manager threads, Stable Queue Transaction Interface threads are started when the Replication Server boots. The Replication Server will start one dedicated Stable Queue Transaction Interface thread for each inbound stable queue and will start one dedicated Stable Queue Transaction Interface thread for each outbound stable queue.

subscription A formal request to receive an initial copy of source data, and to have that copy continually updated in a fully automated manner. You create subscriptions against existing replication definitions, and each replication definition can work concurrently with many subscriptions.

Subscription Resolution Engine Matches transaction rows with replication subscriptions, using (in memory) Replication Server System Database contents. These in memory Replication Server System Database contents are provided to the Subscription Resolution Engine by the Distributor thread. The Subscription Resolution Engine: 1.) Tells the Distributor thread to discard a row if no replication subscriptions match the transaction statement; 2.) Decides what operation to replicate, in order to preserve state consistency; 3.) Decides whether subscription migration is, or is not, required; 4.) Determines which function call to use on the row when applying it to the replicant database; 5.) Attaches the identity, or name, of the destination database to each transaction row that it forwards.

time out After the Replication Server Manager pings a SQL Server, Replication Server or Log Transfer Manager, it waits for an interval of time to decide whether or not the target is up and running. This interval of time is referred to as the time out.

Transact-SQL Stored Procedure An extension to the Transact-SQL language that allows you to bundle Transact-SQL commands and control-flow constructs into a named executable database object.

Transaction Delivery Module Called by the Distributor thread to prepare transaction rows, to be sent to data servers and other Replication Servers. It is the job of the Transaction Delivery Module to package each transaction row as a function call.

user-defined function A Replication Server user-defined function is a function that you create. A user-defined function is a custom-built Replication Server function whose name and parameters are the exact match of the name and parameters of a replicated stored procedure.

user-defined view A user-defined view is a grouping of Replication system icons under a single icon. The purpose of the user-defined view is to organize and simplify the Replication Server Manager Desktop.

USER thread Manages an Open Client login connection from a Replication Server user, typically the Replication Server administrator.

Index

Illustrations are in **boldface**

About the author

Since receiving his M.S. in Management Science & Information Systems from the University of Colorado, Mr. Clifford has, for the past ten years, been designing and implementing distributed client/server systems. Presently, he is working as the Lead Data Architect for a major U.S. firm on Wall Street.

Other Bestsellers of Related Interest

Sybase and Client/Server Computing
Alex Berson/George Anderson
This book contains a practical guide to Sybase system and database design and administration, including guidelines on Sybase installation, hardware, and software requirements; connectivity with mainframe and other databases; backup and recovery; and several sample application programs written for Sybase SQL Server, Net/Gateway, and Open Server.
ISBN 0-07-005203-4 $50.00 Hardcover

Distributed Computing Environments
Daniel Cerutti/Donna Pierson
This book provides a comprehensive look at technical issues, the state of the industry, and the financial implications of using and managing distributed systems in current and future environments.
ISBN 0-07-010516-2 $50.00 Hardcover

Application Development for Distributed Environments
Dawna Dewire
Coverage of such pertinent issues as transaction management and distributed databases; fourth-generation languages, CASE, and client/server tools; product evaluations for ENFIN, ObjectView, PC-XView, HCL-exceed Plus, Desqview/X, MicroFocus AAI, and Forte.
ISBN 0-07-016733-8 $40.00 Hardcover

Client/Server Computing
Dawna Dewire
This authoritative volume covers client/server architecture and its components, client/server applications, and detailed reviews of representative tools used to build graphic client/server applications.
ISBN 0-07-016732-X $40.00 Hardcover

OSF DCE: Guide to Developing Distributed Applications

Harold W. Lockhart, Jr.

Provides a detailed introduction to OSF DCE and each of its major components and a number of general client/server processing models with working example programs, which can be used as a starting point for developing a distributed application.

ISBN 0-07-911481-4 $59.95 Paperback/Disk

Powerbuilder

Joseph Bambara and Paul Allen

All major enhancements of PowerBuilder Version 4 are featured in this guide to the most popular client/server applications development tool. Coverage ranges from PowerBuilder basics to building full-scale systems. How to interface with SYBASE, Oracle, DB2/6000, and other databases is clearly spelled out.

ISBN 0-07-005413-4 $45.00 Paperback